Literary Biography

Literary Biography

LEON EDEL

—

Man is explicable by nothing
less than all his history.
EMERSON

—

Indiana University Press

Bloomington and London

Part of the section on T. S. Eliot in the chapter
entitled "Criticism" is reprinted by permission
of Houghton Mifflin Company from their
anthology *Masters of American Literature*, 1959.

ISBN: 0–253–33540–X (cl.): 0–253–20169–1 (pa.)

To the Memory of E. K. Brown

CONTENTS

Foreword 1973

Literary Biography, which has been out of print since the early 1960's, is being reissued in response to queries that have arisen following completion of my *Life of Henry James.* I had planned to revise and expand this book, but on re-reading it I have come to feel that the original version had an integrity of its own and reflected the spontaneities and enthusiasms of the period when I was in the very thick of a prolonged biographical enterprise. It seems quite proper therefore to let the book stand in its 1959 form even though some of its allusions may no longer apply.

Various critics have asserted that I have made a unique distinction in separating literary biography from other forms. There have been many works on biography in general; but this book's special claim is that it deals with the peculiar problems which arise when a biographer attempts to write the life of an individual who is himself a writer. The problems I set forth in my 1959 preface to the Anchor edition (here retained) are as significant today as they were at that time. I spoke then of bringing literary biography into "mid-century focus" after the discussion opened up by members of the Bloomsbury circle—Virginia Woolf, Lytton Strachey, Maynard Keynes. I think that focus is still needed, and may very well be needed for the rest of the century, for biography continues to be a kind of stepchild of literature. Critics (who are themselves in reality biographers in disguise) often depreciate it; poets and novelists dismiss it fearing revelations of their own lives—which they reveal in every poem or novel they write; and some reviewers assume a condescending tone, usually because their image of a certain subject does not match that of the documented life. But biographies continue to be read and continue to fascinate, and some day—if possible— I hope to expand this work into a full-fledged study. Even in its present modest form it can lay claim to being in the nature of a *poetics* of biography since it is concerned with the biographical finding and making that result in a work of art.

I remember that I wrote the first part of this book in Honolulu during 1955. It makes me aware how long has been my attachment to the form, and how undiminished my interest. I am happy also that this volume now appears in hard cover, for the first time, as well as in paperback.

Leon Edel

The University of Hawaii
March 1973

Preface

This book is composed of material presented originally as a series of five lectures—the Alexander Lectures—at the University of Toronto in 1956. These were subsequently revised and published in England and Canada in 1957; and it is this book, further revised, which now is published for the first time in the United States.

When I was invited to give the lectures, I proposed that these be devoted entirely to the question of biography—literary biography. It seemed to me that this branch of biography had never been sufficiently isolated from the general discussion of the biographical art. I felt that for this purpose my own effort to encompass and re-create the life of a major literary figure—Henry James—would permit me to draw upon personal experience as well as upon those theories which I had found myself putting into practice.

The discourses represent, in effect, more than two decades of reflection upon the questions they project and discuss. Indeed, when I came to prepare them, I found among my books André Maurois's Clark Lectures, *Aspects of Biography* of 1928, in the battered and thumbed French edition I had read and marked long ago in Paris, and Sir Harold Nicolson's Hogarth Lectures, *The Development of English Biography* of 1927, which bore similar signs of study. In surveying the field I discovered that little had been published in recent times about the *theory* of this difficult art, save for certain historical works and occasional essays in learned journals. There had been, in the 1920's, under the stimulus of Lytton Strachey and his friend Virginia Woolf, a healthy discussion of biographical forms. But the Bloomsbury Group disappeared; Strachey died in middle life; his imitators took over his worst mannerisms. The tides of the Second World War closed over Mrs. Woolf, and the great and lively discussion was at an end. So was the wave of biographical writing which distinguished this century's early decades.

My discourses sprang from a feeling that it was time to bring biography into mid-century focus. That they have succeeded in reviving the discussion it may be too soon to say; but it is gratifying to discover in an issue of the *Atlantic Monthly* (current as I write this preface), a leading article on biography, written by Iris Origo, which takes its impulse from my book; and a few weeks ago an article appeared in the literary section of the *Nation* which showed that its author had not only closely read these pages but was himself embarking on a book dealing with literary biography. It well may be that the challenges thrown out to modern biography by Strachey a quarter of a century ago will now be met with greater understanding, for we are coming to recognize his talents and to assess his errors. There is much to admire in him, and we can emulate his method even if his matter was not all that it should be. We know that Strachey displayed his subjects in the dark mirrors of his own antipathies and that this hardly gave him the objectivity we expect of a biographer. But what he said about biographical goals, and what he taught us to do with large masses of material, can still be studied with profit. Too many biographers all too frequently are engulfed by their data; too many card indexes are flung in the face of the public instead of being molded into the semblance of a life.

There is another important reason for a reappraisal of biography at this time. I have been struck in recent years by the attempts of certain critics to rule out biography from the criticism of literature. They argue that we must divorce the literary work from its creator, and while this has led, in a very healthy way, to an insistence upon the importance of a writer's text, it has also led to the view that the literary work is a mere artifact, to be examined as we would a vase or an ancient ornament in a museum. I find it difficult to accept such a dehumanization of literature. The literary voice, after all, is not one of the "voices of silence"; it cannot be separated as easily as might be believed either from the speaker or from the listening world.

The truth is that however much we may isolate a picture on a wall and try to keep our eyes within its frame, we do not wholly lose our awareness of the wall or even of the adjacent pictures; and however much we may look upon a poem, we do not wholly forget the page and the print that gives it visual form, but are concerned also with its audible form and its multiple meanings that spring to life as we read. The reason for this is that we cannot control for one moment all of our inner vision. Our critical imagination has a way of floating around the work that it embraces; we bring into play more involuntary thoughts than we are capable of capturing, let alone controlling. This is a fundamental truth of the critical act. The act can never possess the virginity our "new critics" would like it to have. It persists in remaining a part of something larger—that something we may best describe as the whole study of literature, rather than the mere explication of text.

What has persisted in the minds of critics and explicators is an old-fashioned concept of literary biography to which certain of our biographers still subscribe. This is the belief that it consists of the accumulated card index, the mass of documents from which one is always quoting, and the calendar chronology. In this way they record that part of the daily life of a writer which has practically nothing to do with the making of his works. And Professors René Wellek and Austin Warren are quite right in warning us that such an approach

> ignores quite simply psychological facts. A work of art may rather embody the "dream" of an author than his actual life, or it may be the "mask", the "anti-self" behind which his real person is hiding, or it may be a picture of the life from which the author wants to escape. Furthermore we must not forget that the artist may experience life differently in terms of his art; actual experiences are seen with a view to their use in literature and come to him already partially shaped by artistic traditions and preconceptions.

What these admirable critics are saying, in effect, is that the biography of a writer should be concerned with the imaginative life of that writer. This is quite true; yet they also assume that the writer's imagination is beyond biography's reach and that we can only continue to record external things—dates of publication, what a writer said in a letter, his daily habits of life, his love affairs (or absence thereof), and other "objective" matters.

Criticism will have to learn that it—in itself—is partially a biographical process. The longest section in this book is devoted to the demonstration of this idea which I believe to be fundamental to literary biography. For I am convinced that it is no longer possible for the biographer, writing the life of a writer, to avoid some exploration of his inner life, that part of the artist's life which he lived in the very act of writing, that part which emerges disguised as literature, artfully encased in literary convention, artistic preconception and tradition. I know that it is fashionable for some scholars to dismiss this as "psychologizing," and I recognize that there has been a great deal of rather ineffectual and often misguided literary psychoanalysis of an amateur kind. But why should a psychological speculation, based on carefully gathered data and on observation of repeated patterns in a work, not be as valid as pages of endless and inconclusive speculation about the first night of *Twelfth Night,* or what Shakespeare actually wrote before Falstaff was made to babble of green fields? When we have listened to the writer as he verbalizes feeling in poem after poem or have read him as he brings together his world in novel after novel, is it not possible to risk certain observations about that writer?—may these not be truer than the observations of those who saw him day after day at his club or in various drawing rooms? "Tell me what the artist is, and I will tell you of what he has *been* conscious," Henry James once said. The biographer, functioning as critic and analyst of the work, today might rephrase this: "Tell me of what the artist has been conscious, and I will tell you what the artist is."

In arguing against rigid chronology in literary biography I have found myself criticized by certain colleagues who feel that, in our craft, we cannot allow ourselves the Proustian pleasure of flitting backward and forward in time. I grant them that there must be a chronological progression. This seems to me axiomatic. But I find it difficult to agree with M. Maurois that "It is always a mistake, in a biography, to anticipate. 'This great statesman was born in a small village . . .' No baby is a great statesman. Every man discovers successively the ages and aspects of life." M. Maurois wants us to play a rather curious game of make-believe. When I pick up a biography, I know before I open the book that it is the life of a statesman, of a novelist, or of a soldier—someone who in some way commanded the interest of a biographer. I cannot pretend, as I read on, that I do not know that this baby—say in Stratford-on-Avon—was not just a baby. He was, after all, the baby who was going to write *Hamlet*. And therefore I see no reason why biographers should not move easily through time, and anticipate and tell the story in the very best way they can, forward and backward as Proust moved among his memories and associations. By doing this, as I show in my last discourse, we make a person seem more alive, less an individual living his life solely by the calendar and the clock. The man sitting at seventy for his portrait was once that baby about whom M. Maurois speaks. And that baby was destined to grow into that man who would sit for his portrait in his seventieth year. Our point of departure in the reading of a biography is not necessarily in the cradle, but with the man who achieved greatness, and it is from that greatness that we go back to look at him in his swaddling clothes, attended by the Graces and the Muses—or if he be a figure of evil—by the demons that will mold his life.

The present edition, save for these prefatory remarks, and the passage I have added on T. S. Eliot in the third chapter, is substantially the same as the earlier editions. In the writing of this book I drew, to some extent, upon certain formulations of my ideas concerning biography expressed first in a Moody Lecture at the University of Chicago in 1952 and developed in the preface to *Henry James: The Untried Years* (1953) and the preface to the *Selected Letters of Henry James* (1955); in an article "Time and the Biographer," which appeared in the *New Republic;* and in a B.B.C. Third Program broadcast of 1955. Certain of my formulations were also embodied in an article on biography in the New York *Times Book Review* in 1956. I want in particular to express my gratitude to Professor A. S. P. Woodhouse and his committee who invited me to give the Alexander Lectures at Toronto, and to Morton Dauwen Zabel, who first urged me to speak of my theories of biography when he invited me to Chicago to give the Moody Lecture.

Leon Edel

New York University
14 February 1959

Literary Biography

I Subject

I

Lytton Strachey once described biography as "the most delicate and humane of all the branches of the art of writing." Delicate, I suppose, because the biographer seeks to restore the very sense of life to the inert materials that survive an individual's passage on this earth—seeks to recapture some part of what was once tissue and brain, and above all feeling, and to shape a likeness of the vanished figure. Humane, because inevitably the biographical process is a refining, a civilizing—a humanizing—process. And because it is a delicate and humane process, it partakes of all the ambiguities and contradictions of life itself. A biography is a record, in words, of something that is as mercurial and as flowing, as compact of temperament and emotion, as the human spirit itself.

And yet the writer of biography must be neat and orderly and logical in describing this elusive flamelike human spirit which delights in defying order and neatness and logic. The biographer may be as imaginative as he pleases—the more imaginative the better—in the way in which be brings together his materials, *but he must not imagine the materials.* He must read himself into the past; but he must also read that past into the present. He must judge the facts, but he must not sit in judgment. He must respect the dead—but he must tell the truth. James Anthony Froude sought to tell the truth about the Carlyles and succeeded in bringing down upon his writing table all the hornets of literary London—and of Edinburgh to boot. And yet while he was doing this, other Victorians were being commemorated in large, heavy tomes; they were made to seem not men, but angels, clothed in all the innocence of Adam before the Fall. The biographers who offered the public such gilded statues were considered honorable and truthful men; but candor such as Froude's provoked largely indignation and indeed fright. We deal here in large anomalies.

It is my intention to discuss a specialized branch of biography—the writing of the lives of men and women who were themselves writers. Obviously all the practices and traditions of biography apply to this particular kind of biographical writing: the differences between it and other categories reside essentially in the nature of the subject and corollary questions of emphasis and shading. The biographer of a soldier is apt to be concerned with such matters as strategy and military discipline, the qualities of the military mind, a life of movement and action, indeed all the historic forces that enter into play when we put a soldier into the field. The biographer of a poet is likely to be concerned with literary rather than military discipline, that is, with literary criticism and with the life of the imagination in action. But all biography has this in common, that it is concerned with the truth of life and the truth of experience. How far can a biographer, who by force of circumstances is always outside his subject (and

sometimes decades and centuries removed from it),
penetrate into the subject's mind, and obtain insights
which are not vouchsafed him even in the case of his
most intimate friends? What is the essence of a life,
and how do we disengage that essence from the eternal
clutter of days and years, the inexorable tick of the
clock—and yet restore the sense of that very tick?
Which are the true witnesses of this or that life and
which the false? And how shall a life be written? What
style will best render the life of a literary man who had
some style of his own? And how tell, in especial, the
life of the mind, which is what the literary life really is:
the mind and the emotions—as distinct from the lives of
generals and politicians whose intellectual attainments
were not written out day after day upon sheets of
paper in a study, but were lived out in parliament or
on the battlefield?

I propose to offer first certain general considerations
about the biographer and his subject; and to proceed
thereafter to discuss the quest for materials—that constant search for significant detail, much of it irrecover-
able, which is half the passion of the biographer and
which must occur before he can put pen to paper. And
then we must weigh the relationship between criticism
and biography, for surely the writing of a literary life
would be nothing but a kind of indecent curiosity, and
an invasion of privacy, were it not that it seeks always
to illuminate the mysterious and magical process of
creation. That process belongs to the inner consciousness, those deeper springs of our being where the
gathered memories of our lives merge and in some
cases are distilled into transcendent art. To understand
this we can, in our time, invoke the aid of psychology.
But we must ask ourselves—how useful is psycho-

analysis to the biographer, to what extent may it be invoked?

Finally it will be fruitful to consider closely the relationship the biographer must establish between himself and those clocks which rang the hours in other years. In this fashion it should be possible to formulate a broad concept of literary biography.

II

It is not my intention to venture into the history of biography. It would take us too far afield. There is much to say about the deeply human biographical method of the Gospels and their exalted subject; or about the vivid biographical paragraphs in the Old Testament, so evocative in their brevity, devoted to Ruth and David and Joseph; or about Plutarch, who was concerned with the writing of great lives for the valued ethical generalizations they might yield him. It would be tempting to deal also with the hagiographers, who in their lives of the saints made little claim to science and often even less to veracity, but freely transposed, on occasion, episodes from the life of one saint to another. What was important for them was the example of the saintly life, not the facts of the life itself. My concern here is not with history or with biographies remote in time from us, and so rich a part of our religious and secular heritage. The problem I wish to discuss is the very concrete one of how, in modern times, when we have whole libraries of documents, when tape recorders and films bring to us the voice and the image of the biographical subject—how, in these modern times, biography should be written and by what light of theory we are to work.

4

The interest in the personal and the private life, the life of the inner man, dates in English letters, we might say, from the eighteenth century: certainly it was a harbinger of romanticism. First came the poet, and very much later curiosity about the life of the poet. Had biographical curiosity, or awareness, existed earlier, we would not today be trying to piece together Chaucer's life from those paltry records of his pension and the pitchers of wine bestowed upon him by the royal household. Who would think of writing the life of a modern poet from the record of his check stubs? We write what we pretend is a "life" of Shakespeare from a series of facts which can be set down in a very large hand on a rather small sheet of paper. The Elizabethans had a limited biographical sense; they kept no record of the luminous mind in their midst; but so great is our curiosity that, failing an adequate biography of Shakespeare, certain individuals give him a wholly new life and call him Bacon or the Earl of Oxford.

Modern biography is as modern as the novel; indeed it came to birth almost at the same time. In recent decades there has been a close definition of the craft of fiction, but there has been a singular lack of definition of the craft of biography—and of literary biography in particular. This is not difficult to explain. In the writing of the novel the artist is free to use all the resources of his imagination; in the writing of biography the material is predetermined: the imagination functions only as it plays over this material and shapes it. The art lies in the telling; and the telling must be of such a nature as to leave the material unaltered. The biographer, like the historian, is a slave of his documents. Fewer generalizations are therefore possible. Readers of novels are interested in the problems of storytelling and in theories of fiction; readers of biography take for granted the facts given to them; they are not generally concerned to know how the biographer arrived at them. For these reasons, Percy Lubbock's *The Craft of Fiction* and E. M. Forster's *Aspects of the Novel* continue to be read, while Sir Harold Nicolson's *The Development of English Biography* (I do not speak here of Donald Stauffer's more specialized works) and André Maurois's *Aspects of Biography* tend to be neglected. Yet both Nicolson and Maurois, writing under the fertilizing influence of Lytton Strachey, offered us during the 1920's the liveliest discussion of biography we have had in our half century. The discussion went on around them as well, and we can, if we listen, hear the voices of Strachey himself and of his friend Virginia Woolf, and the group of younger men who learned from them—among them Lord David Cecil and Philip Guedalla. Nicolson reluctantly saw biography as doomed to become a work of science; Maurois argued it could be only an art and should accept itself as such; and Virginia Woolf said it was neither art nor science but a kind of superior *craft*.

Nicolson's survey, which tended to be rather superficial as history, was in reality an essay in definition. He saw biography as "the history of the lives of individual men as a branch of literature" but gloomily predicted that it would eventually become a branch of science. He was writing under the influence of the first popularizations of psychoanalysis a quarter of a century ago and such ephemeral fads as the transplanting of monkey glands. He believed that biographies would tend increasingly to become case histories rather than lives related in literary form. He wrote:

I would suggest that the scientific interest in biography is hostile to, and will in the end prove destructive of, the literary interest. The former will insist not only on the facts, but on all the facts; the latter demands a partial or artificial representation of facts. The scientific interest, as it develops, will become insatiable; no synthetic power, no genius for representation, will be able to keep pace. I foresee, therefore, a divergence between the two interests. Scientific biography will become specialised and technical. There will be biographies in which psychological development will be traced in all its intricacy and in a manner comprehensible only to the experts; there will be biographies examining the influence of heredity—biographies founded on Galton, on Lombroso, on Havelock Ellis, on Freud; there will be medical biographies—studies of the influence on character of the endocrine glands, studies of internal secretions; there will be sociological biographies, economic biographies, aesthetic biographies, philosophical biographies. These will doubtless be interesting and instructive, but the emphasis which will be thrown on the analytical or scientific aspect will inevitably lessen the literary effort applied to their composition. The more that biography becomes a branch of science the less will it become a branch of literature.

Now that we have lived a bit into this future, we can see that Sir Harold's forebodings, for the time being at least, have been groundless. There have been some specialized biographies of the sort he envisaged; their public is limited and they certainly have not supplanted traditional biography. Biographers have continued to write fully aware, as M. Maurois insisted in his book, that man is a volatile creature, that so long as the brain and nerves and the human consciousness defy mechanization, biography cannot be wholly scientific. Virginia Woolf, as I said, took a position rather betwixt and between. The biographer was a craftsman, and on this "lower level," as she put it, he helped to relieve the tension of the world of the imagination: thanks to him sober fact is allowed to intrude upon it.

From our mid-century perspective, I would say that the discussion need not be whether biography is a science or an art or even a craft capable of being learned by any serious, intelligent person. It is a process: scientific when it asks the sciences to elucidate whatever they can about the human being and his personality; an art when it uses language to capture human experience; and requiring all the craftsmanship an individual can command in mastering and disciplining himself to deal with material as rich and varied and mercurial as the mind of man. These are tolerably obvious matters. If you press me, however, I will say that much more art than science is involved in the process, since biography deals with emotions as well as with the intellect, and literary biography with those emotions which give the impulse to literary creation. These, I suspect, we shall never be able to place in a test tube.

III

The biographer is called upon to take the base metals that are his disparate facts and turn them into the gold of the human personality, and no chemical process has yet been discovered by which this change can be accomplished. It is a kind of alchemy of the spirit; to succeed the biographer must perform the unusual—and the well-nigh impossible—act of incorporating into himself the experience of another, or shall we say, becoming for a while that other person, even while remaining himself. This does not mean that he must be an actor. The actor gets into the skin of a character and remains that character on stage, wholly dissimulating his real self. The biographer also is required to get into the skin of his subject; he removes himself sometimes to another age; sometimes he even changes his sex; he takes on another's career, the very wink of his eye or shrug of his shoulder: yet all the while he retains his own mind, his own sense of balance and his own appraising eye. He must be warm, yet aloof, involved, yet uninvolved. To be cold as ice in appraisal, yet warm and human and understanding, this is the biographer's dilemma.

Between the biographer and his subject there is established from the outset a significant relationship—ghostly though it may seem. It is a relationship deeply intimate and highly subjective. I speak of the biographer who selects his own subject as distinct from the one who is writing an official or commemorative biography and who may or may not become emotionally involved with the subject. As a rule the subjective relationship dates from the moment the biographer begins to think about writing a given life. On the surface he has been attracted to this or to that figure for reasons which seem clear enough: he likes the writer's work, or he finds it curious; he may discover some little dramatic fact which serves to kindle the fire, or finds what he knows of the writer's personality pleasing. M. Maurois, in his Clark Lectures, told us much about himself when he described how he came to write the life of Shelley.

In effect he said that he found in the poet a mirror for his own youthful emotions, and "it seemed to me indeed," he wrote, "that to tell the story of this life would be a way of liberating me from myself." This is an illuminating confession. I am sure that if someone were to attempt to study the psychology of biographers, he would discover that they are usually impelled by deeply personal reasons to the writing of a given life— reasons not always conducive to objectivity and to truth. Sigmund Freud, in his probing of the subterranean motivations of man, offered what seems to me a profound warning in his essay on Leonardo da Vinci —a warning to the biographer who ceases wholly to be himself and proceeds not to write but to *rewrite* the life of his subject. As Freud puts it (in the quaint language of his American translator), these biographers became "fixated on their heroes in a very peculiar manner." And he goes on:

> They frequently select the hero as the object of study because, for personal reasons of their own emotional life, they have a special affection for him from the very outset. They then devote themselves to a work of idealization, which strives to enroll the great man among their infantile models, and to revive through him, as it were, their infantile conception of the father. For the sake of this wish they wipe out the individual features in his physiognomy, they rub out the traces of his life's struggle with inner and outer resistances, and do not tolerate in him anything savoring of human weakness or imperfection; they then give us a cold, strange, ideal form instead of a man to whom we could feel distantly related. It is to be regretted that they do this, for they thereby

sacrifice the truth to an illusion, and for the sake of their infantile phantasies they let slip the opportunity to penetrate into the most attractive secrets of human nature.

Freud might equally well have described the opposite of this hero-worshipping kind of biography—the kind in which the biographer selects a subject upon whom he will vent his spleen, not because of any genuine hatred, but because of buried hostilities and unhappy memories which may be fitted to the person selected for vilification.

I think Lytton Strachey had these dangers in mind when he spoke of the biographer's need to maintain his "own freedom of spirit." Another way of putting it might be to say that the biographer must try to know himself before he seeks to know the life of another: and this leads us into a very pretty impasse, since there seems to be considerable evidence that he is seeking to know the life of another in order better to understand himself. The biographer's dilemma thus becomes double: he must appraise the life of another by becoming that other person; and he must be scrupulously careful that in the process the other person is not refashioned in his own image. This, in reality, is the subtle process involved.

But biographers, like their subjects, are human. They do not possess that omniscience which would enable them to see to the very bottom of their own hearts and minds while unraveling the riddle of the heart and mind of another. The best we can hope for, it would seem, is that the biographer should, as Lytton Strachey said, "lay bare the facts of the case, *as he understands them.*" This is obvious enough and yet it is our best—indeed, our sole—answer to the problem of omniscience. Surely a biographer can set forth the data he has gathered and studied only in the light of his own understanding; and his understanding is inevitably a variable, greater or less, depending upon his capacities as well as upon his data. We come round the circle to the basic fact that the biographer can work only by the light of his own intelligence and his own resources. The greater his grasp of reality, the more real his portrait will be. He has taken into his consciousness a great many documents about another's life. And the book that will emerge will be *his* vision, *his* arrangement, *his* picture.

Let us image the great table of biography, for biographers need larger tables or desks than most writers. It is piled high with books and papers: certificates of birth. and death, genealogies, photostats of deeds, letters—letters filled with rationalizations and subterfuges, exaggerations, wishful thinking, deliberate falsehoods, elaborate politenesses—and then, testimonials, photographs, manuscripts, diaries, notebooks, bank checks, newspaper clippings, as if we had poured out the contents of desk drawers or of old boxes in an attic: a great chaotic mass of materials, not to forget volumes of memoirs by the contemporaries—how they abound in some cases!—and the diaries and notebooks of these contemporaries, and often biographies of the subject written by other hands. All this material, assembled out of the years, will make its way into the mind—and the heart—of the man who has gathered it. The death of the owner of many of these documents has tended to level them into a relative uniformity. We can no longer determine whether this particular letter, breathing sweetness and affection, was really written in love, or in pretense of love. The voice that gave it its original inflection is gone; the recipient of the letter is perhaps no longer available to furnish a gloss or to testify what it meant to receive it. Things impalpable surround these palpable objects. The diaries and notes reflecting moods ranging from vexation and anger to transcendent joy, bitter animosity to boundless Christian charity, all had a particular meaning when the author was alive. But once he is dead the meaning becomes more general and uninflected. And the biographer can only absorb these documents into his living consciousness: it becomes, for the time, surrogate for the consciousness that has been extinguished. In other words, the living, associating, remembering biographer's mind seeks to restore a time sense to the mass of data that has become timeless. All biography is, in effect, a reprojection into words, into a literary or a kind of semiscientific and historical form, of the inert materials, reassembled, so to speak, through the mind of the historian or the biographer. His becomes the informing mind. He can only lay bare the facts as he has understood them.

IV

Henry James set down some very eloquent words on this subject—of the change that takes place between the moment when a man is alive, holding the thousands of connecting threads that bind him to the world and his fellow men, and the moment when the threads are suddenly snapped, for all time. "After a man's long work is over and the sound of his voice is still," wrote James, "those in whose regard he has held a high place find his image strangely simplified and summarized. The hand of death, in passing over it, has smoothed the

folds, made it more typical and general. The figure retained by memory is compressed and intensified; accidents have dropped away from it and shades have
ceased to count; it stands, sharply, for a few estimated
and cherished things, rather than, nebulously, for a
swarm of possibilities." There is indeed an extraordinary simplification, and the life that was so rich, so full
of countless moments of experience and emotion, now
is rather disconnected and fragmentary. Let us place
Henry James's words in their proper context. The
novelist was writing of his lately dead friend, James
Russell Lowell. When he set down these words it was
with the image of Lowell in his mind, as he had known
him during more than three decades. The beautiful
commemorative essay which he wrote gives us a vision
of many Lowells—the Lowell to whom James had listened when he was a young man at Harvard, listened
during late winter afternoons when lamps were lit in
the classroom and they illuminated the bearded face,
giving to it a haunted poetic quality; the vigorous
American Lowell in Paris during the 1870's with whom
James supped at a little hotel on the Left Bank before
crossing the Seine, illumined by gaslight which gave
to the water the effect of a varnished surface, to go to
the Théâtre Français; the Lowell of the earlier time
who set down noble lines in memory of the dead, the
young dead, of the American Civil War; and the later
Lowell, the man of letters as diplomat, carrying the
responsibilities of his ministerial post to the Court of
St. James's and into the great houses of Victorian England, the Lowell who lectured the English on the
growth of democracy in America. The "estimated and
cherished things" were those estimated and cherished
by James at the time of Lowell's death in 1891. Yet we,

from our distance, more than half a century later, and many years after James's death, find that time has further summarized Lowell and made him more remote. A certain staleness pervades his writings—they seem bookish and derivative; he has stepped into a greater shadow; at moments he seems to us, in our twentieth-century sophistication, a figure naïve and parochial; he *lives* for us vividly only in some of his essays and lectures and largely when a writer, like James, succeeds in making him vivid for us. What James wrote, in turn, has become one more document— a very beautiful document—one more bit of eloquent testimony to be placed upon the already burdened table of Lowell's biography. The figure of James, along with other of Lowell's contemporaries, has moved into the records of Lowell's life; and the biographer, his task more complex than ever, must himself move among these shadows and documents and "points of view," called upon to sift, to evaluate, to re-create. His task grows in magnitude when he encounters, and places upon his worktable, biographies of his subject written by his predecessors. Here we find we must make still further distinctions—distinctions not often made—between the biographer who writes solely from documents and the one who writes, frequently from a commemorative emotion, having known the dead man. This, very properly, brings us to the name and the example of James Boswell.

V

When Boswell began his preparations to write the life of Dr. Johnson, that great ponderous figure still walked at large, and London still seemed to echo to his conversations and opinions. Boswell found himself in a position of high advantage. For one thing, Johnson believed that "nobody can write the life of a man but those who have eat and drunk and lived in social intercourse with him." What biographer, in Johnson's company, would discourage so genial an opinion? Certainly not Boswell, who therefore had easy and sociable access to his subject. He could listen. He could take notes. He could ask questions.

He could do much more. He could at moments become a kind of organizer and sceneshifter in the life of Dr. Johnson: he could create occasions, incidents, encounters for the life he would ultimately write. This is not to say that he actually arranged Johnson's life for him. The learned doctor was, intellectually, the least passive of men. There were moments, however, when Boswell could, by quiet manipulation, place his subject in a better position for the biographical camera, improve a little on the accidents of life; he could carefully plan—shall we say?—"spontaneous" occasions for the unaware object of his biographical urge. What is disarming in the life he finally wrote, is the candor and innocence with which Boswell describes his own maneuvers and clevernesses. There comes to mind the little episode of the visit to the home of the late Reverend Edward Young, the celebrated author of *Night Thoughts on Life, Death and Immortality*. Johnson was traveling with Boswell and they had stopped at Welwyn, where Young had been rector for more than a quarter of a century. The celebrity-loving, pilgrimage-seeking Boswell wanted to visit the Young house, where the poet's son now lived; and he wanted to do it *with* Dr. Johnson. He feared, however, that Johnson might refuse. Let us see how he goes about his little project:

We stopped at Welwyn, where I wished much to see, in company with Dr. Johnson, the residence of the authour of *Night Thoughts*, which was then possessed by his son, Mr. Young. Here some address was requisite, for I was not acquainted with Mr. Young, and had I proposed to Dr. Johnson that we should send to him, he would have checked my wish, and perhaps been offended. I therefore concerted with Mr. Dilly [their companion on the journey] that I should steal away from Dr. Johnson and him, and try what reception I could procure from Mr. Young; if unfavourable, nothing was to be said; but if agreeable, I should return and notify it to them. I hastened to Mr. Young's, found he was at home, sent in word that a gentleman desired to wait upon him, and was shewn into a parlour, where he and a young lady, his daughter, were sitting. He appeared to be a plain, civil, country gentleman; and when I begged pardon for presuming to trouble him, but that I wished much to see his place, if he would give me leave; he behaved very courteously, and answered, "By all means, Sir; we are just going to drink tea; will you sit down?" I thanked him, but said, that Dr. Johnson had come with me from London, and I must return to the inn and drink tea with him; that my name was Boswell, I had travelled with him in the Hebrides. "Sir, (said he,) I should think it a great honour to see Dr. Johnson here. Will you allow me to send for him?" Availing myself of this opening, I said that "I would go myself and bring him, when he had drunk tea; he knew nothing of my calling here." Having been thus successful, I hastened back to the inn, and informed Dr. Johnson that "Mr. Young, son of Dr. Young, the authour of *Night Thoughts,* whom I had just left, desired to have the honour of seeing him at the house where his father lived." Dr. Johnson luckily made no inquiry how this invitation had arisen, but agreed to go, and when we entered Mr. Young's parlour, he addressed him with a very polite bow, "Sir, I had a curiosity to come and see this place. I had the honour to know that great man, your father." We went into the garden, where we found a gravel walk, on each side of which was a row of trees, planted by Dr. Young, which formed a handsome Gothick arch. Dr. Johnson called it a fine grove. I beheld it with reverence.

The scene has been set, the visit arranged. Boswell now can listen to Johnson discourse upon the subject of Dr. Young. The insatiably curious Bozzy has, for the occasion at least, satisfied his curiosity and succeeded in his stratagem. The learned doctor seems to enjoy himself; the deception has been harmless enough. And the episode illustrates for us the striking advantages an energetic biographer can enjoy when he is master not only of documents but of living situations, and when his subject is within easy and friendly reach.

But Boswell not only set his living scenes; he often gave direction to the conversation within them. He was free, indeed, to discuss even the subject of biography with his biographical subject.

Talking of biography, I said, in writing a life, a man's peculiarities should be mentioned, because they mark his character. *Johnson.* "Sir, there is no doubt as to peculiarities: the question is, whether a man's vices should be mentioned; for instance, whether it should be mentioned that Addison and Parnell drank too freely: for people will probably more easily indulge in drinking from knowing this; so that more ill may be done by the example, than good by telling the whole truth."

And Boswell goes on to attempt to reconcile this view with an opposite view expressed by Johnson on another occasion.

> Here was an instance of his varying from himself in talk; for when Lord Hailes and he sat one morning calmly conversing in my house at Edinburgh, I well remember that Dr. Johnson maintained that "If a man is to write *A Panegyrick,* he must keep vices out of sight; but if he professes to write *A Life,* he must represent it really as it was:" and when I objected to the danger of telling that Parnell drank to excess, he said, that "it would produce an instructive caution to avoid drinking, when it was seen, that even the learning and genius of Parnell could be debased by it." And in the Hebrides he maintained, as appears from my *Journal,* that a man's intimate friend should mention his faults, if he writes his life.

I cannot take seriously Johnson's "varying from himself in talk"—Boswell's graceful euphemism for contradicting himself—to which the biographer makes allusion. It gives an impression of the play, back and forth, of an active mind, and perhaps even of tongue in cheek. We cannot know, inevitably, when Johnson used a tone of irony; we can no longer catch the precise inflection of his voice; and I am not at all certain that Boswell, ingenious and clever though he was, was always capable of catching *tone*. But we do know that whatever he may have said in his conversations, Johnson insisted emphatically in his writings upon truth and upon psychological insight in the handling of biography. "There are many," he wrote in the *Idler* of 24 November 1759, "who think it an act of piety to hide the faults and failings of their friends, even when they can no longer suffer by detection. We therefore see whole ranks of characters adorned with uniform panegyric, and not to be known from one another but by extrinsic and casual circumstances." And he added that "If we owe regard to the memory of the dead, there is yet more respect to be laid to knowledge, to virtue and to truth." Johnson followed his own counsel in his *Lives of the Poets*, perhaps with an excess of idiosyncrasy and sometimes a want of critical judgment. But it is easy to forgive him, for he strikes a blow for biographical truth and he himself was aware that idiosyncrasy is a part of character, and character makes for individuality in biography. "A blade of grass is always a blade of grass," Johnson told Mrs. Thrale; "men and women are *my* subjects of inquiry."

Boswell set scenes; he sometimes set the course of the conversation; and he boasted openly and truthfully that he made the life of his man of letters more lively, and therefore ultimately more readable:

> In the evening we had a large company in the drawing-room, several ladies, the Bishop of Killaloe, Dr. Percy, Mr. Chamberlayne, of the Treasury, &c. &c. Somebody said the life of a mere literary man could not be very entertaining. *Johnson.* "But it certainly may. This is a remark which has been made, and repeated, without justice; why should the life of

a literary man be less entertaining than the life of any other man? Are there not as interesting varieties in such a life? As *a literary life* it may be very entertaining." *Boswell.* "But it must be better surely, when it is diversified with a little active variety—such as his having gone to Jamaica; or—his having gone to the Hebrides."

"Johnson," adds Boswell after this flattering—and self-flattering—allusion to the tour of which *he* was the chief architect, "was not displeased at this."

And so we can see how Boswell helped to *live* the biography he was ultimately to write; it was he who, on occasion, introduced that "little active variety" into the career of the literary man he had chosen as his subject—or as the mirror to his own prodigious vanity? For we might ask, as we read on, where, in this amazing work, does biography begin and autobiography end? We have seen how Boswell managed to be both behind the scenes and within the talk, genially and busily intrusive, ubiquitous friend, ubiquitous biographer. Perhaps intrusive does not sufficiently describe his Johnsonian activities, for we know that on one occasion, when he was cross-examining a third person about Johnson—and in Johnson's company—the doctor became understandably impatient. "You have but two subjects," he thundered at Boswell, "yourself and me. I am sick of both."

There was, for instance, their little journey undertaken early in 1776. On page after page Boswell gives us those fine everyday details which make Johnson come alive for us at every turn. Yet there are moments, such as when Boswell suddenly begins to have anxieties about his family in London, which, strictly speak-

ing, have nothing to do with the life of Johnson.
Boswell tells us: "I enjoyed the luxury of our approach
to London, the metropolis which we both loved so
much, for the high and varied intellectual pleasure
which it furnishes"—and the inimitable Bozzy here
makes us pause. We wonder: is Boswell traveling with
Johnson or Johnson with Boswell? He adds: "I experienced immediate happiness while whirled along with
such a companion." We do not, indeed, begrudge Boswell his happiness so long as he keeps his companion
in sight; and we are happy enough to be in the presence of his own extraordinary self. But the biographer,
coming upon the scene more than a century later, finds
that he must ride in the coach not only with the subject
but with the former biographer! Indeed, the former biographer, in more instances than can be counted, man-
ages to step squarely in front of his subject.

When death finally ended the busy life of Dr. Johnson, his disciple, friend, companion, admirer set down
his monumental record from a vast long-gathered ar-
chive, documentary and reminiscential. Boswell wrote
out of close observation; he wrote also from records,
as we have seen, sometimes deliberately created—mirrors deliberately held up to catch the reflection of
the living Johnson. Singlehanded, in this fashion, he
created the first great modern biography. Sir Harold
Nicolson has very happily contrasted biography before
and after Boswell as the difference between a series of
studio portraits (or a succession of lantern slides) and
the cinema. "Boswell," said Sir Harold, "invented actuality; he discovered and perfected a biographical
formula in which the narrative could be fused with the
pictorial, in which the pictorial in its turn could be
rendered in a series of photographs so vividly, and

above all so rapidly, projected as to convey an impression of continuity, of progression—in a word of life." But we must observe that Boswell was aided in his invention of actuality in biography because Dr. Johnson was *actual* to him. For the fact remains that he did know his subject for twenty-one of his seventy-five years; and while it has been estimated that during these twenty-one years, representing one third of the adult life, he was in Johnson's company on two hundred and seventy-six days, or less than one year, he nevertheless knew a palpable Dr. Johnson; and he knew other persons who knew a palpable Dr. Johnson. He had access not only to his subject but to the subject's wide circle of friends. If he invented actuality, he in some ways invented, or "created," Dr. Johnson as well; or if that be too extreme a way of putting it, let us say that he created lively stage sets and adroit stage directions for the drama he was to write. His book speaks for his power and his assertiveness as a biographer; at the same time he has committed his successors to shifting from point of view to point of view, not only coping with the subject, but puzzling out a large series of mirror images, some with as many distortions as the mirrors in a fun house at a fair.

VI

The biographer who works from life, as Boswell did, has an extraordinary advantage over the biographer who works from the document, whether he plays sceneshifter or not. He has seen his man in the flesh, he has been aware of a three-dimensional being, drawing breath and sitting in the midst of an age they both share. In his mind he retains a sharp image of his subject. He has heard the voice and seen the gesture (and even in our age no recording, no cinema picture can provide a substitute for that). The latecoming biographer hears only the rustle of the pages amid the silence of the tomb. This is explanation enough for the fact that the greatest biographies in our literature have been those which were written by men who knew their subjects and who painted them as the painter paints his picture—within a room, a street, a landscape, with a background and a context rich with its million points of contemporaneous attachment. Boswell, Froude, Lockhart, Forster, repose upon our shelves with vividness and mass and authority which later biographers cannot possess.

But the later biographers have quite an opposite advantage, that of greater objectivity gained from wider perspective, their time distance which Sir Max Beerbohm so comfortably described in his lecture on Lytton Strachey: "the past is a work of art, free from irrelevancies and loose ends . . . the dullards have all disappeared. . . . Everything is settled. There's nothing to be done about it—nothing but to contemplate it and blandly form theories about this or that aspect of it." The biographers who knew their subjects in life began with a certain picture of the man they had known; they had a conception of his personality and an image to which documents might be fitted. The documents might, in some cases, alter the image for them, but this does not change the fact that in re-creating it they shuttled from life to the document and then from the document to life. The biographer of the long-dead subject shuttles from one document to another: he begins and he ends with his documents. He is obliged to spend much of his time in trying to form, in his mind, that image which his predecessor possessed, so to speak, "ready-made." He labors to visualize its aspect, its style, its manners. Not having the testimony of his own eyes, he finds he must use the testimony of others; and then he discovers that the testimony is often contradictory and invariably colored by individual points of view. But again, precisely this awareness of contradictions may give the distant biographer a marked advantage in his search for the truest picture.

There is then always this peculiar relationship between any biographer and his subject. The biographer undertakes to capture—or to recapture—mirror images, and he must be careful not to reflect a subject in a mirror which is too much himself. Long before he will have to indulge in this dual analysis of subject and self, he must discover the materials out of which his biography will be written. They must be gathered in a strange and often compulsive quest upon which every biographer embarks with a single-mindedness which makes him look into every book index for the mention of his subject and keeps him browsing endlessly in libraries. He enters a labyrinth, the exit of which he cannot know. At the beginning his great worktable is comparatively bare. Long before he has emerged from the maze it will be cluttered with more material than he can ever use; or it may remain so bare that he has virtually no story to tell—save a tale of general bafflement. I want to describe this journey through the biographical maze, this passionate quest, during my second discourse.

II Quest

I

We have seen that readers tend to be more interested in how a piece of fiction or a poem came to be written than in the genesis of a biography. They are aware that the biographer is a kind of Sherlock Holmes of the library; they know that he has delved and traveled and asked questions and read many books. They are nevertheless interested not in the writer of the life, but in the life itself. The delights of the search, the uncovering of documents, the discovery of persons who have outlived their time and can still put the biographer into relation with a "visitable past"—these belong to the joy of biographical re-creation which the reader is unlikely to want to share. The emotion, or shall I say the passion, of the search must, by the very nature of the biographer's task, be reconverted into a dispassionate account of the life. The peculiar satisfaction of unearthing a fact must take second place to the importance of the fact itself. I know indeed of only one significant biography which has succeeded in focusing attention not upon the story itself, but upon the story of the story.

I allude to A. J. A. Symons's fascinating little book

The Quest for Corvo. Symons discovered, in gathering
the materials for the life of the unfortunate Rolfe, or
Baron Corvo as he styled himself, that the hunt was
much more exciting than the life he had to tell. The
life itself was that of a minor writer with illusions of
grandeur who had a facility for making friends, borrowing money from them, and then quarreling bitterly
with them. The situation is not unfamiliar. He used to
involve himself in lengthy disputes which resulted in
vituperative letters and unsavory episodes. Because
of his petulant and quarrelsome nature, Rolfe could
never maintain any semblance of a relationship with
publishers; his books were scattered, his papers were
difficult of access, and his ornate manuscripts, written
as if by a monk in a monastery, were much sought after
by collectors. The man was a minor figure indeed in
the world of letters, although he had crossed the path
of certain figures of larger stature in the 1890's.

Symons decided, in the circumstances, to write the
story of Baron Corvo's life not as a conventional biography, but as some hunter might describe the story
of his adventures in the jungle; or a detective the
step-by-step deductions, the encounters, and coinci-
dences which led him to his goal. So Symons tells the
story of his search for manuscripts and the tracing of
letters, the people he met, the survivors who had
known Corvo during his last depraved days in Venice
and those who had glimpsed him earlier, during the
phase when he believed he had a vocation for the
Church and wrote his fantastic daydream, *Hadrian
VII*, in which he imagined himself elected Pope. In the
process, Symons had to tell us about Corvo, but always
as the subject of the hunt, and from the narrative we
gain a rather interesting picture, between the lines, of

the meticulous Symons himself and his interest in the rococo of literature. It is a story of the hunter as well as of the hunted. Biography and autobiography genially merge in this unique work, quite alone in the tolerably long list of English biographies of our time. Symons appropriately subtitled his book "an experiment in biography."

II

I have already spoken of the choice of subject and how it touches the subjective life of the biographer. In a literary biography the initial impulse, more often than not, has been a response to the writer's work, to those three voices of poetry T. S. Eliot has described which are in reality different inflections of the one voice. Whether the poet speaks to himself or in the role of a character, he speaks, in fine, to us, his readers. Biographical curiosity, more often than not, begins in this way: what sort of man, we ask, is addressing us, and how and why did he come to say the things that he is saying? We are not, after all, in the habit of listening to disembodied voices, although sometimes the voice itself is sufficiently powerful to hold our attention and by its very strength commands us to listen and to understand. The biographer recognizes soon enough that in the study of literature the voice and what it says are almost inseparable: a voice which can be heard above the world's tumult usually possesses highly individual qualities of resonance and depth, or delicate lyricism, or even a certain compelling stridency, with varied shadings of which it alone is capable. We can always recognize it as peculiar to the one person—and to no other. This is what we mean when we speak, in literature, of style.

Once the search begins for the story of a life—or of a style—which has been speaking to us through a poem or a novel or a play, the record is largely that of a kind of unrelieved obsession, of long hours in libraries, of correspondence with many people in distant places, of searches for old manuscripts in out-of-the-way muniment rooms, not to speak of delicate negotiations with surviving wives or husbands and relations and literary executors. Sometimes the mass of the material is overwhelming. Neither one large table nor even a large room suffices. Indeed there is at Hyde Park in New York an entire library housing the materials for the life and times of Franklin Delano Roosevelt, and I am sure it would take a library as large or larger to house all the materials of Sir Winston Churchill's crowded life. Lockhart found himself burdened with a great weight of papers when he came to write the life of his father-in-law, Sir Walter Scott. The biographer of Thomas Wolfe will have to cope with several tons of documents now in the Houghton Library at Harvard. We live in an age in which our biographical subjects are more conscious of the meaning of history than their ancestors, and perhaps, at times, too acutely and self-consciously aware of the possible claims of posterity. I hesitate to think of what lies ahead: when the biographer will find confronting him radio transcripts, recorded telephone calls, and tape recordings of interviews, as well as film strips and kinescopes preserving television appearances. The time may yet come when biographers will work not alone, but in large, well-organized teams, in order to encompass the weight of paper and plastic that modern man leaves behind him. And often it is the lesser scribbler who accumulates the most papers; his work is perhaps not sufficient to give him a hold on posterity, and he hopes to do it by sheer poundage. Professor Norman Holmes Pearson of Yale has made public a letter from Hervey Allen which showed an extraordinary solicitude for the biographer.

I am a very methodical person in regard to records and correspondence [the author of *Anthony Adverse* wrote to Professor Pearson]. Over the years there has been an unbelievable number—thousands—of letters from people all over the world, literary and otherwise, and these have all been kept in carefully annotated and organized files, together with the replies. Amongst these letters are quite a number from most of my contemporaries. In addition to that, there are all the manuscripts of the several books, and the complete story of their publication,—reviews, comments, and all that goes with it. . . . I am now engaged in arranging for a shed in which to store this material . . . and get it all together with the correspondence of the war years, and the publication of books that have taken place since. In other words, to get the whole mass of material together and properly arranged in its sequence of monthly and yearly files. . . . Part of this is forced upon me because I must have, easily available and on hand, the records of the past years, in order to satisfy the Internal Revenue Department, which is forever pestering me with questions that must be completely and intimately answered as to why I did certain things in the past. As at the present time I am paying income taxes and agents' fees etc. etc. in some twenty-one countries, you can see how complex it is, and yet how necessary.

Posterity may not be altogether as happy as the Internal Revenue Department for such deference; yet what biographer or historian would want to apply the match of kindness to this shedful of papers? An announcement I once received for an exhibition of the manuscripts and papers of Sinclair Lewis read: "Lewis undoubtedly had a realistic attitude towards his own position in American letters, for he made the task of future biographers and chroniclers *easy* [the emphasis is mine] by preserving preparatory notes for his novels, every important manuscript in *all* stages, as well as much of his literary correspondence." Easy! The writer of these words has obviously never tried to write a biography. It is true that the biographer, like an historian, always wants more documents than he can ever use, and I am sure Mr. Mark Schorer, working among the Sinclair Lewis papers, has felt himself endowed with an embarrassment of riches; at the same time he must experience, on occasion, an overwhelming revulsion against such paper madness. Boswell boasted in the opening pages of his life of Johnson that he had not melted down his materials, but had allowed his subject to speak wherever possible in his own voice. Imagine the twentieth-century biographer, groaning under his burden, making such a boast! If he followed Boswell's prescription he would have to write a massive life and what publisher—what reader, indeed—would want it? Rare are the lives in the history of the world that require such amplitude. Even Masson's *Milton* crowds the shelf as a history of Milton's time as well as of his life; and the Monypenny and Buckle *Disraeli* or the Nicolay and Hay life of Lincoln, splendid in their many-volumed detail, are become source books, from which other biographers write the readable single-volumed lives.

We have a striking paradox when we contemplate the biographer rich in material of his subject and his starved brother handling material of the pre-biographical era. The latter would give much for a few ounces of documents on the life of Shakespeare or of Marlowe. The former, an unwilling glutton, busy shoveling tons of paper, at moments longs for a leaner diet. Who is to say, however, which has the harder task: the biographer starved of detail who must grub for his facts in the entire background of an era, or the one for whom the background is not even visible because detail clogs the foreground? There seems to be small choice; either way the past looms as a rough mountain, difficult of access. I suspect that if one were to measure the hours of work and the reward, it would be discovered that biography is the costliest of all labors on this earth.

III

There is still another kind of subject for the hard-working biographer, the exact opposite of the hoarding, accumulating type who can't throw papers away. The opposite kind would seem to have had a fireplace in every room of his house, the more quickly to get rid of papers. I have an example ready at hand and I shall invoke the honorable precedent set by André Maurois, who ventured at some length into his personal biographical problems during his Clark Lectures at Cambridge. I think I can describe the quest for the materials of Henry James's life with an intimacy no one can duplicate; and I suspect that this intimacy is preferable to my drawing upon examples at second hand from other biographers. I shall risk the charge of being frivolous and autobiographical in the interest of the generalizations I wish to draw. I would particularly justify my choice of Henry James on the ground that he offers us the unique picture of a novelist who, in the most premeditated fashion in the world, arranged a tug of war between himself and his future biographer.

Let us look first at the problem of James's letters.

The novelist wrote for fifty years. Few days passed without the regular stint at his desk; even when he traveled, his pen set down its record in journals, travel articles, tales, novels. At the end of his day's writing there was the dinner, the social evening, the theater, and then a late return and letters—it might be ten or fifteen in an evening—to friends, relations, acquaintances. Sometimes he wrote full warm letters largely about his art. He wrote gossipy letters as well, but he seldom talked about himself. He could be very precise and matter-of-fact in writing to editors, publishers, or literary agents. He was equally precise and acutely critical and honest if literary matters were being discussed. Concerning himself, however, the details are always general and often trivial: the intimate glimpses are few and rather guarded. His letters are remarkable for their fluency, their cordiality, their vitality; they are the overflow of a man's creativity, the surplus of his genius. They are often highly descriptive and they are nearly always filled with fine free phrases thrown off with the greatest of liberality. He accepts an invitation: "Dearest Clare, You should have heard the peal of strident laughter with which I greeted—and treated —your question of whether I shall really turn up on Friday next; a question so solemnly and so sacredly settled in the affirmative, an intention so ardently cherished, a prospect so fondly caressed. . . ." He issues an invitation: "Dearest Jocelyn, If you are miraculously

34

able to come—on the 7th and to sit through my twaddle, to feel you beautifully there will give all the pleasure in life and be an immense support, to your all-affectionate old Henry James." He describes a voyage: "I was lifted over the wide sea in the great smooth huge kind Mauretania as if I had been carried in a gigantic grandmother's bosom and the gentle giantess had made but one mighty stride of it from land to land"; or a wedding, in "a very cold church, to see my friend Mrs. Carter, married: a rather dreary occasion, with a weeping bride, a sepulchral clergyman who buried rather than married her, and a total destitution of relatives or accomplices of her own, so that she had to be given away by her late husband's brother." Or he finds the elegiac words with which to mourn his old friend, Fanny Kemble: "I am conscious of a strange bareness and a kind of evening chill as it were in the air, as if some great object that had filled it for long had left an emptiness—from displacement—to all the senses." He thanks a distinguished authoress (Sara Orne Jewett) for sending him her book: "It would take me some time to disembroil the tangle of saying to you at once how I appreciated the charming touch, tact and taste of this ingenious exercise, and how little I am in sympathy with experiments of its general (to my sense) misguided stamp. . . . There I am—yet I won't do you the outrage as a fellow craftsman and a woman of genius and courage, to suppose you not as conscious as I am myself of all that, in these questions of art and truth and sincerity, is beyond the mere twaddle of graciousness."

The mere twaddle of graciousness. So many of Henry James's letters were that, a distribution of accolades and muted strictures, a wrapping of sharp criticism in the soft cushions of kindness. James's letters can be very misleading. Their extravagant affection sometimes suggests closer friendship than actually existed; their elaborate, friendly irony masks deeper feelings, an intention to express the truth at all costs and yet to pad it out with gentle words. Read in isolation or out of context, these letters are sown with pitfalls. Elaborate praise in one sentence is often offered as prelude for sharp criticism; a verbal pat on the back sometimes becomes a subterfuge for a sound boxing of artistic ears. It is only by a long and careful process of study of the different qualities of friendship expressed in hundreds of James's letters—I should say thousands, for I have read some ten thousand—that I have found it possible to sort out the exact meaning of his relationships with his correspondents and to isolate from the "mere twaddle of graciousness" those communications which speak for the more intimate Henry James. He was conscious early of the claims of posterity. He often enjoined his correspondents to "burn this, please, burn, burn." I find these particular words in a letter to his sister Alice. The fact that I am able to quote them indicates what happened. Few lit the destructive match. Nearly everyone preserved Henry James's letters.

I find them on all sides: one turned up in Honolulu recently, another in Finland. And each owner, even today, a generation removed from the recipients, seems to discern in them particular qualities, confidential and intimate. Yet how deceptive this can be! For in this biographical abundance much more is concealed than is revealed. The letters are a part of the novelist's work, of his literary self, a part of his capacity for playing out personal relations as a great game of life . . . but we find indeed that only a part of James's life is in them, especially when we compare them with the letters of the romantic poets, those who tore their passions to tatters, in particular on the Gallic side of the Channel. Not so in the letters of the American novelist: we seem indeed to watch him as he watches himself in a mirror.

A man so cautious left no love letters: at least so far none have been found; indeed a man so cautious apparently did not allow himself to be in love. And when a man is as self-concealing as this, where is the writer of his life to find him? The biographer is confronted with the most elaborate and most organized game of hide-and-seek or hunt-the-author ever conceived. James's deliberate effort to thwart his future biographer can be discovered on every side. "Artists," he wrote when he was twenty-nine, (three years before he completed his first novel), "artists as time goes on will be likely to take the alarm, empty their table drawers and level the approaches to their privacy. The critics, psychologists and gossip-mongers may then glean amid the stubble." Three years later, when his first novel is being serialized in the *Atlantic Monthly*, he returns to the same theme: "A man has certainly a right to determine what the world shall know of him and what it shall not; the world's natural curiosity to the contrary notwithstanding," and he adds that there should be a "certain sanctity in all appeals to the generosity and forbearance of posterity, and that a man's table drawers and pockets should not be turned inside out."

What steps did Henry James take to keep his table drawers and pockets from prying biographical hands? For one thing, he had a secret drawer in his desk: but when it was discovered after his death it yielded a gout remedy and a prescription for eyeglasses! Wherever he turns, the biographer stumbles upon an ironic mockery, a kind of subterranean laughter—at the biographer! Henry James is coy in his prefaces about the magazines in which his work first appeared. He revises his early writings and alters the first person "I" to the more general "one." He hedges certain passages of his autobiographies with qualifications. The euphemism becomes a constant instrument of expression. And then there is the direct attack upon the past.

Early in the new century James's health gave him some concern. One day he heaped his correspondence of forty years upon a great roaring fire in his garden at Lamb House, in Sussex, and watched its progress from paper to ash, obeying "the law that I have made tolerably absolute these last years as I myself grow older and think more of my latter end: the law of not leaving personal and private documents at the mercy of any accidents, or even of my executors! I kept almost all letters for years—till my receptacles could no longer hold them; then I made a gigantic bonfire and have been easier in mind since." Like his own character in *The Aspern Papers,* he could have boasted, "I have done the great thing." The "great thing" was the burning of the Aspern papers, the love letters of the famous poet, one by one, in the kitchen stove. It is quite clear that Henry James, warming his hands by the fire at Lamb House, would have exclaimed with Dickens who lit a similar blaze at Gad's Hill: "Would to God every letter I have ever written were on that pile." But think of the irony: while Dickens and James, both prolific letter writers, burned letters that would have illuminated many other lives and done service in other biographies, they could do little about those which illuminate their own and which today turn up in such numbers.

Henry James was acutely conscious of having lived into the new age of journalism and its excessive curiosity about the living great. His private life was private indeed. He could push secrecy to a fine art. He confided in no one. His open, ritualistic life was a mask, and in a late essay on George Sand he repeated in more elaborate form what he had said as a young man and also embodied in one of his late ghostly tales, *The Real Thing*. This tale has a biographer-hero who in the end finds the ghost of his subject planted in the doorway of the study, warning him to abandon his project. In the essay on George Sand, James deplores —and not without some relish—the manner in which that prolific lady's love affairs were unscrambled in public and the way in which her letters of passion, and those of Chopin and Musset, were given to the world. At the same time a mischievous and slightly boastful note creeps in. He would be careful not to reveal himself. No one would turn *his* pockets inside out.

He begins the essay by observing that to leave everything to the biographer, to make his task easy, was, so to speak, to remove one's clothes to the public gaze, and when one had laid bare one's life, as George Sand and her biographer had done, what was there left to know? "When we meet on the broad highway the rueful denuded figure we need some presence of mind to decide whether to cut it dead or to lead it gently home, and meanwhile the fatal complication occurs. We have *seen*, in a flash of our own wit, and mystery has fled with a shriek." He goes on to say that the writer does suffer accidents, he can't hide all his secrets, and there are many kinds of encounters on the broad highways of literature and life. What is to be done? With that need for putting everything in order—the house of fiction as the house of life—Henry James suggests that the biographic quest be organized. "The general guarantee in a noisy world," he says, "lies, I judge, not so much in any hope of really averting them [the encounters] as in a regular organisation of the struggle." The subject of a biography has in the past left things too much to luck. It is up to him to create the ground for a more equal conflict. And he continues:

> The reporter and the reported have duly and equally to understand that they carry their life in their hands. There are secrets for privacy and silence; let them only be cultivated on the part of the hunted creature with even half the method with which the love of sport—or call it the historic sense— is cultivated on the part of the investigator. They have been left too much to the natural, the instinctive man; but they will be twice as effective after it begins to be observed that they may take their place among the triumphs of civilisation. Then at last the game will be fair and the two forces face to face; it will be "pull devil, pull tailor," and the hardest pull will doubtless provide the happiest result. Then the cunning of the inquirer, envenomed with resistance, will exceed in subtlety and ferocity anything we to-day conceive, and the pale forewarned victim, with every track covered, every paper burnt and every letter unanswered, will, in the tower of art, the invulnerable granite, stand, without a sally, the siege of all the years.

The tower of art, the invulnerable granite, the siege

of the years: this is Henry James's challenge to posterity—and to his biographer!

IV

Every track covered, every paper burnt, and subtlest
twist of all—every letter unanswered! We are offered
by such a stroke the absolute, the deathly silence of the
tomb. One can attempt to match wits with covered
tracks and burnt papers, but out of silence there can
come only—silence. And yet not all papers do get
burned; not every track can remain covered; not every letter can remain unanswered. The subject of a
biography may throw up roadblocks, but he can never
completely stop the traffic—any more than can the
biographer.

There exists, for instance, a monograph on angina
pectoris by the late Sir James Mackenzie, who was not
only one of the greatest of England's authorities in the
field of heart ailments, but a wise and gifted healer. His
little book, written for the members of his profession,
is the last place in the world that we would look for
biographical material concerning an American novelist. Yet in this medical volume, never intended for
literary biographers, I one day found the following passage to which I was led by a clue that had quite
fortuitously come to me. The passage is worth quoting
from beginning to end:

I was once consulted by a distinguished novelist.
Just before he came to see me I had read one of his
short stories, in which an account was given of an
extraordinary occurrence that happened to two children. Several scenes were recounted in which these

children seemed to hold converse with invisible people, after which they were greatly upset. After one occasion one of them turned and fled, screaming with terror, and died in the arms of the narrator of the story. After my examination of the novelist I referred to this story and said to him "You did not explain the nature of the mysterious interviews." He at once expounded to me the principles on which to create a mystery. So long as the events are veiled the imagination will run riot and depict all sorts of horrors, but as soon as the veil is lifted, all mystery disappears and with it the sense of terror.

I tapped him on the chest and said "It is the same with you, it is the mystery that is making you ill. You think that you have angina pectoris, and you are frightened lest you should die suddenly. Now, let me explain to you the real matters. You are sixty-six years of age. You have the changes in your body which are coincident with your time of life. It happens that the changes in the arteries of your heart are a little more advanced than those of your brain, or in your legs. It simply follows that if you be more judicious in your living, and give your heart less work to do, there is no reason why you should not reach the ordinary span of human life." He was greatly cheered by this way of putting the matter and remained in good health, except that his powers of locomotion became more restricted and he died at the age of seventy-two from cerebral embolism.

Now the description of the story sounds very much like *The Turn of the Screw* and the explanation of how to keep events veiled and allow the reader's imagination to "run riot" corresponds to Henry James's descrip-

tion of his formula for "horror" and evil in his preface
to that ghostly tale. Moreover, James's correspondence
shows that in 1909 he became extremely worried about
his health and consulted physicians, and this year fits
the doctor's description of his novelist patient's age,
sixty-six. Also we know that Henry James died at
seventy-two of cerebral embolism. But the novelist
might reply to us: "You have no absolute proof!"—and
he might say other rather forceful things as well about
the biographical invasion of the privacy of the consulting room. "You have no absolute proof," he might say,
"for I am not mentioned by name." Well, it so happens
that there is proof which comes as close to being absolute as any proof can. Discreet as Sir James Mackenzie
was, his case history (Case 97), buried in this volume
among many other such histories, did not escape, during the 1920's, the eye of Dr. Harold L. Rypins, a professor of medicine in Albany Medical School, with a
penchant for literary study. Dr. Rypins wrote a letter
to Sir James, pointing out that the novelist had been
dead for several years, and inquired whether the secrets of the consulting room, already partly divulged,
might not be further unveiled. "You are quite right,"
replied Sir James in a letter which I have seen, "and
it was *The Turn of the Screw* to which I referred. After
our first interview we became very friendly and he
frequently visited me, particularly when depressed."

Every track covered?

In his memoirs Henry James describes how he
moved into a little room near Harvard in 1862 when
he was nineteen and began to write with the hope of
being published. Then, with his characteristic coyness
in such matters, he throws these words at his biographer: "Nothing would induce me to name the peri-

odical on whose protracted silence I had . . . begun to hang with my own treasures of reserve to match it." James seemed to believe that his early writings were beyond recovery. Did not anonymity provide a sheltering cloak? Would it not cast a perpetual doubt for any future wielders of the bibliographical pickax and spade? He little dreamed that nearly all his anonymous contributions to the *Nation*—book reviews, travel articles, and literary notes—would some day be known because an account book, listing payments for articles, would be preserved by one of the *Nation's* editors. But exasperating evidence began to appear in recent years that buried prose existed, written before those articles were discovered in 1907 by Le Roy Phillips in his *Nation* researches. Among the papers relating to Henry James's brothers I found a letter from Garth Wilkinson James of December 1864 written from the Civil War front to the elder Henry James saying: "Tell Harry that I am waiting anxiously for his 'next.' I can find a large sale for any blood and thunder tale among the darks." And long ago T. S. Perry, the friend of James's adolescent years, testified that the would-be novelist wrote early tales in Newport in which the heroes were villains and the heroines were positively dripping lurid crimes and seemed to have read Balzac in their cradles.

Publication in 1950 of James's letters to Perry offered further evidence. In March of 1864, a year before the appearance of James's first signed story in the *Atlantic Monthly*, the novice in letters was writing to Perry that the printer's devil had been knocking at his door. "You know a literary man can't call his time his own." The literary man added that he was sending a story to the *Atlantic* and giving Perry's address as the place to which the acceptance or rejection would be sent. "I cannot again stand the pressure of avowed authorship (for the present) and their answer could not come here unobserved. Do not speak to Willie of this." If Henry James's sensitivity to fraternal teasing is here revealed—"Willie" being his elder brother, William James, who was to become the eminent psychologist and philosopher—there is also revealed an important fact: avowed authorship—"again."

But where, in what strange waters, is the biographer to fish for this avowed author? Remember, "Nothing would induce me to name the periodical," Henry said, half a century later. The exasperated biographer or bibliographer can only set such things aside and hope for some happy accident. Meanwhile there are always other problems. One was to obtain certain letters I had long wanted, written to a Venetian hostess, an American lady, who was for many years a friend of Henry James's and of Robert Browning's. I had learned that they were in possession of that lady's daughter, aged ninety-two, who lived in a renaissance palace in Florence. These elements sound rather like Henry James's own tale of *The Aspern Papers*. But unlike the "publishing scoundrel" of that story, I was unable to journey to Florence and sit on the doorstep of the modern Juliana in the hope of obtaining a glimpse of the letters. Instead I invoked the good offices of a relative of the Florentine lady who lives in New York and who was on her way to Italy.

Weeks elapsed. I completed the manuscript of my biography of Henry James's early years and cleared my cluttered table preparatory to cluttering it again with the materials for the second volume—but with an acute sense that there were certain loose ends perhaps never to be properly tied together. One day I received a tele-

phone call. My ambassadress had returned. She had
copied certain letters for me. I saw, on reading them,
that they would serve my later needs. But during my
talk with her she quite casually mentioned that her
grandmother had lived in Newport and had been a
neighbor of the Jameses. She had found her grandmother's letters to her father. Did I think there might
be material for me in this correspondence? She would
look through the accumulation, one never could tell
what an old bundle of letters might reveal. And so it
was that early one November morning, when my manuscript had already been dispatched to my publisher,
I received another telephone call from this amiable
and helpful lady. She had found a solitary reference
to young Harry James in her grandmother's letters and
she read from a letter dated 29 February 1864: "Henry
James has published a story in the February Continental called a Tragedy of Errors. Read it." Thus an
old letter, written by an unobtrusive bystander, a
Newport neighbor, to her son, divulged what nothing
would have induced the novelist to divulge. The *Continental Monthly,* in its bound volume at the New York
Public Library, was as crisp and new as if published
yesterday. Sure enough, a story called *A Tragedy of
Error,* unsigned, appeared in the February 1864 issue,
a month before James spoke of his avowed authorship.
It fitted Perry's description and Wilky James's; it was
lurid blood-and-thunder stuff; it was seasoned with
those French phrases Henry delighted in using during
his formative years; it was set in France; the heroine
was sufficiently Balzacian—or perhaps had a George
Sand touch about her: in theme, style, substance, it is a
primitive Henry James story.

Every track covered?

See then by what circuitous routes we travel in the biographical maze; a chance encounter in a drawing room with the widow of the Albany doctor led me to the letter from Sir James Mackenzie; an appeal for certain Venetian letters brought me a much more valuable Newport letter. Such are the vicissitudes of the quest, and if there are unwritten letters—or unanswered letters—there appear to be letter-writing neighbors. Perhaps the cunning of the inquirer is ferocious, as Henry James said; but let us remember that the art of the biographer does not lie wholly in the uncovering of tracks. The particular skill of Sherlock Holmes, you will remember, in the days before fictional detectives became sadists and resorted to violence and blackmail to solve crimes, lay not so much in observing the bits of mud on the boots of the visitor, or evaluating an interlocutor from his habits of dress, or reading between the lines of what he was saying. It lay in his power of deduction, his imaginative grasp of his materials, his ability to deduce the unknown from the known. So the biographer must not be content to be merely Sherlock Holmes, the sleuth. He must possess Holmes's capacity for synthesis and ratiocination. To stumble upon James's visit to the consulting room of Sir James Mackenzie was a rare bit of luck; but it is what transpired between James and Mackenzie, and how it relates to James's work, that is important, and unless the necessary connections are made, all that we have is a rather charming anecdote. To have stumbled on the anonymous story is but a lucky accident, due to chance as much as to persistence. The meaning of that story, its value to us as part of James's late adolescence, or as art, partake of the essential task of the biographer. The mass of documents on the worktable remains a mass, inert, paper and words, to which we have added but one more document by uncovering this particular track. It is the arrangement of these documents and their distillation into a homogeneous, synthetic whole that provide the real test of modern literary biography in the sense in which I think it should be written.

Did the discovery of this early story make necessary any change in my book, since I had already completed it when the happy accident of its finding occurred? The question should be answered. *A Tragedy of Error* is about a strong, determined Frenchwoman who takes a lover during her husband's absence in America and who, on learning of his impending return, plots with a fisherman to have him drowned.

"You want me to finish him in the boat?"
No answer.
"Is he an old man?"
Hortense shook her head faintly.
"My age?"
She nodded.
"*Sapristi!* it isn't so easy."
"He can't swim," said Hortense, without looking up, "he—is lame."
"*Nom de dieu.*" The boatman dropped his hands.

A writer's first story is often more transparently auto-biographical than his later work. In this case I had only to insert a brief analysis of the tale at the proper chronological moment. It confirmed my original decision to devote the early pages of the book to a more detailed account of the elder Henry James's lameness than had hitherto been given—he lost a leg when he was thirteen—and to show how deep an impression the father's accident had made on his son; and also how the son's vision from childhood had been of a father who, for all his vividness and charm, was a vacillating individual while his wife gave an impression to her children of a strength and determination almost masculine. That understanding had been arrived at earlier from a reading of James's work. The citadel of granite *had* yielded these observations. The new track uncovered confirmed, for an earlier stage, what is quite apparent in later evidence. The pattern of the work had yielded a pattern of the life.

And this brings us to the next problem in our inquiry into the nature of literary biography. The pile of documents has now been assembled. Great quantities of paper have been set aside as of little use. The essential diaries and writings, the important letters and notebooks, everything that throws light upon the character and the personality and the artistic imagination, is there for us to use. The writer's works have been closely read and reread—the biographer is always reading them, he can never have enough of them. Now in particular the biographer's critical faculties come into play. They have been operative all the time, inevitably, as he has gone through his materials. But in the process of sorting, arranging, preparing to write, he must be ready to function as a critic of literature as well as a literary historian. He is called upon for an awareness of certain standards, a feeling for form, and an understanding of the nature of the work itself. He must also have a profound understanding of what constitutes testimony, what may be held to be valid and invalid. He has been interrogating clouds of witnesses almost as if he were a studious lawyer bent not upon prosecuting anyone, but on arriving at the truth. This, the question of the biographer's function as a critic of literature and of historical evidence, becomes the subject of our next discourse.

III Criticism

I

The material is gathered. Our great table, piled high with documents, confronts the biographer. On his shelves he has assembled, row upon row, the works of the writer whose life he wishes to recover and to place within a book. Sometimes there are only a few works, as with James Joyce, and sometimes, as with poets, there is only the slim volume of verses. Strange thought in such instances: that there should be such a weight of paper to surround the single book—one thinks of John Keats in particular—so much material to set beside the impalpable, evocative words by which the poet has crystallized experience, his associations of several or of many years, into a few simple lines, a series of verses that lie so lightly within the hand.

How different is the task of the critic, especially the "new critic"! His table, in contrast to the biographer's, is uncluttered. No birth certificates, no deeds, no letters, no diaries, no excess literary baggage: only the works, the poems or the novels or the plays, to be read and reread, pondered and analyzed, in a high clear literary light, a communion between words and print and a critical intelligence, greater or less, as intelligences go. The critic, when he is performing an exclusive function of appraisal, need not be a biographer, although there are few critics who do not cast at least a sidelong glance at a literary life. The literary biographer, however, must at every moment of his task be a critic. His is an act of continual and unceasing criticism.

The task begins with the reading and evaluation of the work of his subject; it extends to that other form of criticism, the weighing and evaluation of evidence, a function quasi-legalistic or juridical, requiring hard-headed logic, a good sense of reality, and an imagination perhaps akin to the poet's, although functioning in matters at times rather prosaic. Both forms of criticism are not in reality divorced from each other: they function simultaneously and call for a constant and studious watchfulness.

II

The critical reading of the works involves for the biographer a complete knowledge of them; he must steep himself in them until he can offer an explication of every text; he must be aware of the way the author uses the materials of his craft and appreciate formal structure and the relation of work to work; he must possess and cultivate all the sensitivities of the critic and what we might call the *critical* imagination. The critic and the biographer must see the particular and the general, the story itself and the myth of which it may be a part; they gather up the images and symbols of the poet, or in fiction the design, the range, the matter, the manner, the creation of characters, their projection and their relations—gather them up to attach them to tradition and discipline and influence, and determine their essential pattern and meaning. In a word, the biographer enters into the heart of each piece of writing as if it were the only work ever written; and as he reads and studies it he relates it to the consciousness that gave it birth and to the world in which that consciousness functioned. He discovers recurrent images and recurrent modes of thought; patterns have a way of repeating themselves, for each writer has his own images and his own language and his own chain of fantasy; there is no writer, no matter how rich and varied his imagination, who does not possess his individual world of words and his peculiar vision of reality. One need not venture far into the earlier T. S. Eliot to discover how often dry bones and windy spaces, rats and desiccation spring from his vision into his verbal structure, and how characteristically he sees streets and cities and the people within them. There is no poet or prose writer who forges a style and achieves transcendent utterance without stamping his effigy on both sides of every coin he mints. A style, it has been said, is a writer's passport to posterity. This is another way, I suppose, of saying that the style is the man. The biographer can thus argue, with equal validity, that the man is the style. Indeed this is what he is always trying to show.

In this reading of the works in a fashion as closely critical as that of any of our most addicted critics, the biographer reminds himself, in the light of the twentieth century's exploration of the psyche, that every comma, every period, every inflection, every word has been placed on the page by the living, glowing, creating consciousness. If he reads the words of the novelist, he soon begins to see that certain types of story— regardless of the adventitious circumstances of creation

—certain significant characters, certain solutions, and certain ethical views have a way of recurring, always in new and artful disguises. However much a great work is independent of its creator, and may be judged independently, invisible threads remain—many more than anyone can discover and disentangle—which bind it to the fashioning consciousness. There is a little story which charmingly illustrates this elementary point, so important in explaining the biographical approach to art and to life. It is that of a young woman who in the early dawn dreamt that the wrapped and silent figure of a man came to the foot of her bed and stood looking at her. Her alarm was great. And as she drew the bed-clothes about her with—one may well imagine—trembling hands, she fairly screamed: "Oh my goodness, what are you going to do to me?" Whereupon the figure broke his stony silence to reply, without moving: "I don't know, lady. It's *you* who are having the dream."

We dream our own dreams: no one else dreams them for us, no one else puts them into our heads. Indeed everything we put into the dreams, however brilliant or absurd, pleasant or painful, is the work of our own inner imagination. When a writer sits down to write, all his past sits behind his pen. His muscles and his nerves, and above all his emotions—and no one else's—drive the pen across the page. And this one self driving the pen is many selves, some of them very contradictory. "A biography is considered complete," observed Virginia Woolf, "if it merely accounts for six or seven selves whereas a person may well have as many thousand." Yes, but we must remember they all belong to the one person: and it is this person who is sought by the biographer.

Mrs. Woolf, who wrote many wise words about the

art of biography, also observed that "every secret of a writer's soul, experience of his life, every quality of his mind is written large in his works, yet we require critics to explain the one and biographers to expound the other." There is a rueful note in this coupling of critics and biographers, the note of a writer who would have the work be all-sufficient—beyond criticism, beyond biography—but who is well aware that this cannot be. Virginia Woolf was expressing a wish and compounding an irony rather than asserting the inviolability of the artist's work. It is illuminating, however, to ask ourselves, in pondering her words, why the critic and the biographer are needed, since their function is precisely to pluck out "every secret of a writer's soul" and rob the work of all its mystery. They tend to make it as plain and as clear as daylight, so that the reader may appreciate its complexity and through understanding come to experience it all the more deeply. *Every secret of a writer's soul, every quality of his mind.* The act of imaginative writing is an act of expression as much as an act of communication. The inner promptings to which a writer listens cannot remain within; they seek an issue, they must emerge; and they usually do in the form of narratives—prose, lyrical, dramatic—tissued out of past experience and formed in a literary tradition. So long as these suggest the secrets of a writer's soul and the quality of his mind, as they must, the curious reader, sharing the writer's experience, will want to learn the secret and pierce to the heart of the mystery.

"In our opinion," wrote Henry James, "the life and the works are two very different matters, and an intimate knowledge of the one is not at all necessary for the genial enjoyment of the other. A writer who gives us his works is not obliged to throw his life after them, as is very apt to be assumed by persons who fail to perceive that one of the most interesting pursuits in the world is to read between the lines of the best literature." To read between the lines of the best literature can indeed be one of the most absorbing pursuits in the world: to catch the flickering vision behind the metaphor, to touch the very pulse of the hand that holds the pen—this is what the biographer attempts, although he knows that at best he will capture only certain moments, and largely echoes. The critic reads to expound and expatiate upon the words that issued from the pen: the biographer does this always to discover the particular mind and body that drove the pen in the creative act.

I knew once in Paris a very old lady who had been a minor poet among the Victorians. She used to sit at eighty near the smiling portrait of herself painted by Sargent when she was twenty and talk, in the years between the two wars, as if she had seen Browning the day before yesterday and as if Walter Pater had tipped his hat to her that very morning when she opened her shutters and saw him passing in the street. In the preface to her collected poems, A. Mary F. Robinson, whom I knew as Madame Duclaux, wrote: "My life has been an Ode, of which these pages are scattered fragments. If ever I have escaped from its tranquil sequences, it has been but for an instant and through some partial opening of the gates of Imagination, set in movement by some incident in real life, or some episode of my reading. I have never been able to write about what was not known to me and near." This is vivid testimony from a woman of great sensitivity and of strong literary impulse, to the invisible ties that bind a poet to his poems.

With a major poet such as William Butler Yeats, his testimony is written large in his works. Many of his poems are autobiographical: more than half a hundred, set down over as many years, are inspired by his frustrated love for Maude Gonne; and constituting a veritable gloss to the poems are his remarkable *Autobiographies,* which provide them, as one critic has said, with "a heavy scaffolding of biographical information." Yeats dedicated the biographies "to those few people mainly personal friends who have read all that I have written." These words suggest that he felt the testimony of the *Autobiographies* to be no less a part of the poet than the poems themselves. This seems to me to be the burden of his *Ego Dominus Tuus:*

> The chief imagination of Christendom,
> Dante Alighieri, so utterly found himself
> That he has made that hollow face of his
> More plain to the mind's eye than any face
> But that of Christ.

"There is always a living face behind the mask," Yeats once wrote in his diary. This is another way of saying that there must always be, inevitably, a poet behind a poem.

III

The first type of criticism practiced by the biographer, then, involves a full examination of the substance, the aesthetic qualities, the very fiber of a work of art in the attempt to recover the mind and the pulse-beat of its creator. Of the second type of criticism—the judicial—

there is much that could be said. It is of a more technical order. The biographer is called upon to impose logic and coherence upon the heterogeneous mass of facts he has assembled, recognizing that in the life he is pursuing they seemed quite arbitrary and, on occasion, illogical. Mrs. Woolf felt distinctly that biographers were inclined to be excessively compulsive. She speaks of that "riot and confusion of the passions and emotions which every good biographer detests." I think that she is mocking even more than mere biographical tidiness. She is criticizing biography for its failure to engage itself sufficiently in the emotional life of its subject; she believes that it concerns itself too much with those dry facts which we can read in condensed form in any Who's Who or the biographical dictionaries. John Masefield had some similar thought in mind when he set down the following lines:

> When I am buried, all my thoughts and acts
> Will be reduced to lists of dates and facts,
> And long before this wandering flesh is rotten
> The dates which made me will be all forgotten;
> And none will know the gleam there used to be
> About the feast-days freshly kept by me,
> But men will call the golden hour of bliss
> "About this time," or "shortly after this."

The Poet Laureate, like Mrs. Woolf, seems to feel that biographers are rather prosy individuals. But is it really true that they do not seek the gleam and the golden hour? I think a good biographer is not afraid of emotion or passion. But being a good biographer he knows how elusive they can be, how transitory and shadowy; he knows that a passion held up under the yellow lamplight on his worktable amid the paper mountains tends to look rather tame and perhaps overlogical, which passion seldom wants to be. And it requires endless ingenuity on the part of a biographer to discover the emotion of his subject after it has coalesced into the poetic phrase or been transferred to a group of characters in a novel.

There is no moment of emotion in all biography, I suppose, more fully expressed than Rousseau's description in his letter to Malesherbes of his great illumination, the central illumination and turning point of his life: the sudden upsurge of feeling which told him that men are by nature free and that it is society which puts fetters upon this freedom. This was, indeed, the great *frisson* of the romantic movement. Rousseau wrote to Malesherbes many years after the experience, telling how he set out one day to walk to Vincennes to visit Diderot, who was then in prison. Reading a newspaper as he strolled along, he came upon an announcement of an essay contest. The subject was whether the arts and sciences had corrupted civilization. The title suggested a train of thought of the most inspiring kind. Rousseau himself did not remember all the details. He knew only that he was overcome by feelings so powerful that at this moment it seemed to him he had touched eternal truth. "Suddenly I felt my mind dazzled by a thousand flashes of enlightenment; swarms of vivid ideas presented themselves to me with a force and confusion which threw me into a state of indescribable turmoil. I felt overcome by a giddiness resembling intoxication." When he emerged from this ecstasy of divination he was sitting under a tree. He had wholly lost himself in his great reverie and had no sense of how long he had been there. The tears were streaming down his face; his shirt front was wet from the salt bath it had received.

All this is to be found in the letter to Malesherbes. It is a riot and confusion of passion and emotion which no biographer in his right mind could detest. The episode speaks too much for life, it challenges the imagination, it is far too human and extraordinary to be anything but the most vivid kind of material. Yet the biographer cannot take such a letter at its face value, though he will hardly want to ignore it. Even if it is fictitious, the incident remains a very pretty piece of fiction, and it is set down in the hand of the immortal Jean Jacques. Various persons did indeed express doubt about the authenticity of Rousseau's account; they felt that he had embellished things rather excessively. Diderot himself, no longer as friendly with Rousseau as he had been at the time of the episode, claimed that when Jean Jacques came to the prison they merely discussed the essay. Rousseau's latest biographer, Professor F. C. Green, was faced here with a task of judicial criticism. He had the text of the letter to Malesherbes: he had the disparagement of Diderot, as well as other memoirs which directly accused Rousseau of falsehood. This was difficult evidence to weigh. But Professor Green shows us that most of the accusations stemmed from Diderot, who knew that he was not gently handled by Rousseau in a part of the *Confessions* then unpublished; and Diderot naïvely admitted he was challenging Rousseau to "forestall the effects of a great calumny." Diderot's version of the scene at Vincennes was that, consulted by Jean Jacques, he advised the latter to take the line no one else would take in the essay contest, to which his friend remarked "*Vous avez raison.*"

"It is much more probable," writes Dr. Green, "that

Rousseau had already decided to take the line he did, and that Diderot approved, not necessarily because he believed that the arts and sciences had corrupted modern civilization, but because he loved a controversy. Now," and here Professor Green reaches the culminating point of his reasoning, "at no time does Diderot deny that Rousseau arrived in a state of agitation and that is the decisive point. For why on earth should Jean Jacques have been so excited if he had merely resolved to defend the banal and orthodox alternative?"

I have not given all the details of Professor Green's reasoning and have rather rudely torn this passage from a closely argued context: but I am interested in showing how a biographer is constantly forced to analyze and reason, to deduce and to speculate. Nor is his task completed when he has held up to the bright light of reason claim and counterclaim, as in this instance. There remained for Professor Green still one more question, and that the most important: what was the nature of Rousseau's high emotion, whether actual or invented? To arrive at the answer Professor Green had to know the whole man; by carefully matching early experiences out of Rousseau's copious *Confessions* with other available data he reached the conclusion—admittedly speculative—that the title of the essay had touched an old chord of memory "at a critical moment in his psychological existence," and it was in reality not the intellectual process provoked by the essay theme, but a flood of old and deep associations and memories which led to the flood of tears.

What really happened on the road to Vincennes we can never know. That moment, so highly personal and subjective, seems lost forever save as Rousseau himself preserved it, although his account is circumstantial enough, despite the ambiguous testimony of the others. What the biographer has accomplished by functioning as critic of certain biographical texts has been to show how this "riot of passion and emotion" fits into the pattern of Rousseau's life and is consistent with it.

IV

"There is always a living face behind the mask." If we accept Yeats's words and think of the poet's life as inextricably woven into his works, it becomes difficult to take the rigid view of certain of our critics who demand an absolute divorce between biography and criticism. They have stated their arguments in a rather extreme fashion, perhaps in justifiable reaction to the way in which some writers and teachers tend to talk around a text and to substitute biography and literary history for it. I will grant them without hesitation their claim that biography need not affect critical evaluation—although there are times when it does make for richer evaluation. When Samson, in Milton's tragedy, says:

O dark, dark, dark amid the blaze of noon

he is speaking for his creator's darkened state as for his own. And when Professor Douglas Bush describes this as "impersonal art charged with personal meaning," he is offering a critical observation infinitely richer and more truthful than that of the critic who, ruling out biography, confines himself to discussing exclusively the verbal felicity and rhetorical power of the line I have quoted. Mr. Cleanth Brooks, in defining the position of the modern or the "new" critic, has said: "Modern critics tend to force attention back to the text of the

work itself: that is, to look at the poem as a poem, not
as an appendage to the poet's biography, nor as a reflection of his reading, nor as an illustration of the history of ideas." To force our attention back to the text is
a good thing; the close reading of that text is the
beginning of all literary study; but it is not the end of
it. The text cannot be an "appendage" to the biography
of the poet, for it is an integral part of it; and it is a
reflection not only of the poet's reading but of his way
of experiencing life. And certainly sometimes it may
illustrate the history of ideas as well. It seems to me
that no critic can read a poem without calling upon
his reading of other poems—how else is he a critic?—as
well as his stores of accumulated feeling and knowledge, historical, biographical, psychological, philosophical, which exist in his consciousness, so that any evaluation or judgment he pronounces is, in fine, colored by
his whole emotional and cultural past, as much as the
poet's was colored by his when he wrote his poem.

I am inclined to think that the "modern" critics are
trying to narrow down the critical act far more than is
necessary, and to achieve a kind of "pure" criticism
possible only through a species of self-delusion, in the
process of which the critic equates himself with the
common reader. Even as no historian could write the
history of France without looking into Germany, so no
critic, I hold, can explicate—the very word implies this
—anything without alluding to something else. T. S.
Eliot clearly and admirably stated this for us in his
discussion of the function of criticism:

> Comparison and analysis need only the cadavers on
> the table; but interpretation is always producing
> parts of the body from its pockets, and fixing them

in place. And any book, any essay, any note in *Notes and Queries,* which produces a fact even of the lowest order about a work of art is a better piece of work than nine-tenths of the most pretentious critical journalism in journals or in books. We assume, of course, that we are masters and not servants of facts, and that we know that the discovery of Shakespeare's laundry bills would not be of much use to us; but we must always reserve final judgment as to the futility of the research which has discovered them, in the possibility that some genius will appear who will know of a use to which to put them.

Mr. Eliot goes on to say that fact cannot corrupt taste and that the real corrupters are those who supply opinion or fancy. The votaries of opinion and fancy would do well to hearken to the biographer who can materially assist them. For faced with modern art—the surrealist poem, the abstract painting, the intricate composite symbolism of works such as *Finnegans Wake* —criticism finds itself admittedly forced, sometimes in a rage of bafflement, into speculation or inarticulateness. When art becomes abstract to this degree the author is speaking wholly from his private world and in his private language; and any critic who tries to read his meaning by any other process than the biographical indulges in guesswork and creates his own work of art upon the edifice of the other: he projects his own feelings and can discuss only his relationship to the work. Where abundant material is available the biographer can offer a reasonably clear understanding of the creator, and our understanding of that personage should make his work more intelligible. For only by ascertaining what the symbols meant to the artist in such instances can we hope to arrive at an accurate deciphering of his symbolic code.

V

Certain critics insist that any attempt to relate biography and the artist's work, and in particular any attempt to read the life of the creator in his books, constitutes a "biographical fallacy." Reflecting this view, Professors René Wellek and Austin Warren have said that "the poem exists, the tears shed or unshed, the personal emotions, are gone and cannot be reconstructed, nor need they be." The biographer, I think, is inclined to dissent from such a view. He holds that the personal emotions have not necessarily vanished and that at least a portion of them may be recovered and may perhaps be found to have some relevance. I do not think that most biographers have as naïve a concept of their craft or art as that imputed to them by Mr. Frank H. Ellis, who, in a long paper in the *Publications of the Modern Language Association* some time ago, embarked upon the task of trying to dissolve the *Elegy Written in a Country Churchyard* into Gray's life, and on finding he could not do this announced the "biographical fallacy" to have been proved. I think all that Mr. Ellis proved was that he was a rather inexperienced biographer. "Biographical experience," he wrote, "can no more be reconstructed from a poem than the poem (if it were lost) could be reconstructed from the experience." Well, we know that the parts are never equal to the whole. I am aware that what Mr. Ellis was trying to say was that some biographers take too many liberties: they read a writer's work as if it were his internal monologue or stream of consciousness, or use letters as if they expressed the truest feelings of their author. Certain biographers do tend to read too much out of a work, and this is just as false as the effort of certain critics to read too much into it.

In selecting Gray's *Elegy* for his laboratory experiment, Mr. Ellis tried to discover, as he put it, "the extent to which Gray's experiences actually figure in the poem." The question, inevitably, is what Mr. Ellis means by "experience." He has no difficulty in showing us that all the things Gray did during the period of the writing of the poem tell us very little about it. If ever poem were written that illustrates how a total experience sits behind the poetic pen, this one would seem to offer a perfect illustration, and to have done full justice to his experiment Mr. Ellis should have invoked Gray's entire life. The experiences he seeks out are all of the matter-of-fact kind and have little to do with the emotions without which any discussion of so remarkable a poem is impossible. That the elegy was not written in a country churchyard, that it cannot be determined whether the poet actually sat in the "yewtree's shade, where heaves the Turf in many a mould'ring Heap," Mr. Ellis goes to great pains to show: but no biographer would be so naïve. It is easily demonstrable that Gray read *Lycidas*, addicted student of literature that he was; he understood what he could do with the elegiac form. Mr. Ellis writes that "the churchyard is not Stoke Poges, which was by no means a 'neglected spot,' was barely within sound of the Windsor Castle bells, had only an inconspicuous tower, and probably had no yew-trees." To such literalness does he commit us. He seems worried also as to whether a yew tree can cast a shadow by moonlight, but does not seem to have been sufficiently experimental to venture out on a moonlit night to see for himself, as any puzzled biographer might do if he felt he needed this information. While I recognize that some biographers have tried to place Gray among the headstones, spontaneously inditing a poem over which he worked in reality for several years, I would submit that Mr. Ellis is looking almost wholly away from the biographical process.

A skilled biographer writing Gray's life would be concerned with the elegiac emotion and quality of the poem and would not quibble over the little unprovable facts. He might want perhaps to know whether Gray had strolled through a churchyard at some time or other and sat in the shade of a tree, whether yew or otherwise; the timing of the experience is not relevant: indeed he could take all this for granted—the poem's testimony seems amply sufficient on this score. Much more significant is Gray's need to write on this theme —common enough in poetry—of the transitory nature of life, of the muteness of the multitude, of the general sadness of love. Where does life lead? Is all vanity? What hope is there for man? Crucial for the biographer is whether the poem is merely a conventional exercise in such melancholy or whether it reflects an actual state of depression which drove Gray to meditate upon death. The biographer, like the critic, must concern himself with the predilection for the crepuscular, for churchyard and ivy, and night birds among the poets who were to follow; he may see in the eighteenth-century Gray a foreshadowing of the romantics. And yet the poem's diction, and the manner in which the thoughts are given, speak not for romanticism, but for the classical frame and the classical tradition. The poem is romantic in its melancholy and its personal tone; but it is as rational as its century. There is more of

Milton and of Pope in it than there is any foreshadowing of Wordsworth. And it is when we look at the
simple facts of Gray's life that we discover evidence
enough of churchyards and graves. Death was known
to him as intimately as it can be to any man. The poet
had survived eleven brothers and sisters; and as
Joseph Wood Krutch has suggested, we might indeed
speculate about the deep melancholy implicit in the
inscription Gray caused to be written on his mother's
grave—"the careful tender mother of many children,
one of whom alone had the misfortune to survive her."
Indeed when Gray died, his testament asked that he
be buried in his mother's tomb. He never married. He
lived a life so withdrawn and so little self-assertive that
he published his celebrated poem only when it became
necessary to prevent its being printed by pirates. Here
are explanations enough for the muted tone, the
mourning for "inglorious Miltons," the quality of feeling that pervades the *Elegy* for all its adherence to
literary convention. Mr. Ellis's attempt to reduce the
poem to biography in terms of particular churchyards
and yew trees can only be considered a travesty upon
biography. If one works from the poem to life, it must
be through the choice of subject—Gray's choice—and
what he projected into it. And I think that a skillful
biographer who had no details of Gray's life, reading
the poem for the first time, would be able to recover
from its tone and mood the poetic emotion and the
quality of mind of the poet, so largely written into it.
He could not recover *actual* biographical detail; he
would, for instance, find in it no evidence of the great
loss Gray suffered, a few months before he began writing the poem, in the death of his friend of many years,
Richard West; but what he would find expressive of

Gray—find it by the process of induction—is the important part of the poet's life: the passive, quiet individual, bookish, learned, given to reverie and self-consolation, a good Christian, a melancholy man who holds that all is vanity, that the path of glory, as of obscurity, leads but to the grave, and who has sought and found the "cool sequestered vale of life."

We have had to glance rather superficially at Gray, about whom serious biographical works have been written, but with which I am not at this moment concerned. What I wished to show was that if there be a "biographical fallacy" it is a protest against the biographical misuse of a writer's work which was very common two or three decades ago; and that if a work cannot be redissolved into a life, it can offer us something of the—shall we say?—*texture* of that life. Nor is there anything particularly novel in this view: the question has been debated for a very long time indeed. It has been given relevance only because in putting forward the "biographical fallacy" certain critics have too hastily rejected biography altogether. The best statement I know on behalf of the biographical approach to criticism was made by a man who, I suppose, by some of the current definitions, would be considered no critic at all: I allude to Sainte-Beuve. He set down a long time ago certain words which seem to me to sum up entirely what I have been trying to convey. They can be found in the second of his *Causeries* on Chateaubriand, in the third volume of his *Nouveaux Lundis:* "Literature, literary creation, is not distinct or separable, for me, from the rest of the man. . . . I may taste a work, but it is difficult for me to judge it independently of my knowledge of the man himself; and

I will say willingly, *tel arbre, tel fruit*. Literary study leads me thus quite naturally to the study of the mind."

VI

Tel arbre, tel fruit. The tree may indeed be discovered by its fruit; and I am prompted—so important do I consider this question—to pursue the matter further. It has been comparatively easy to glance at Gray, about whom several biographies have been written. How, it might be asked, would I proceed in the case of a contemporary writer whose works we have, but whose life is unknown to us? How much of T. S. Eliot's life—his "inner" life—is discoverable in his work? He serves our purpose admirably. No biography of him has been written. We have lived for years with his essays and poems; we have seen his plays; he is very much in our midst, active, celebrated, honored. We have listened to his recordings; many of us have heard him give readings and have gazed upon his countenance, which he has described—in terms of his cat's view of himself—as having a grim brow, a prim mouth, and features of clerical cut. This may be the self-portrait, but what portrait can we sketch from a critical reading of his works? Certainly it is possible to make a few general observations.

We know, for instance, from Mr. Eliot's preface to *For Lancelot Andrewes*, that he has thought of himself as having the views of a classicist in literature and a conservative in religion and politics. We are led to observe, however, on reading his poems and plays, that he has been anything but classical and conservative in his creativity. He may place a dark and rigid frame around his poetic canvas; yet the canvas itself belongs distinctly to the era of Picasso, or might even be likened at times to the strange, polished creations of Salvador Dali, in which battered and bent clock visages are scattered amid dry bones and rocks on endless sand in a timeless and arrested world. There are moments indeed when one wonders whether Dali is not painting illustrations for *The Waste Land* and *The Hollow Men.*

The real face of T. S. Eliot looks out at us from his poems as neither prim nor clerical, certainly not as the stanch and on occasion even platitudinous defender of orthodoxy. We may find in his poems a New England puritanism which speaks for rigidity; but there is also a paradoxical defense of everything the Puritans fled. The royalist in politics is on the side of the rebels in art, the twentieth-century experimenters of the avant-garde. The Anglo-Catholic in religion may be the author of a series of meditations on the Lambeth Conference of the Church of England; this has not kept him from writing a preface to a novel, about Parisian prostitutes and pimps called *Bubu of Montparnasse.* The religious moralist is also a realist.

This double identity, the Eliot of conformity and religion and the Eliot of artistic revolt, can best be understood if we recognize that we have in him a creator who is also a critic. In this he resembles his fellow-American Henry James. And what enabled both to exercise these double functions was that they incorporated conservatism and tradition into their experience of life, and were so settled and secure in this that they could be bold enough to alter it. James was virtually unique in his character as novelist-critic; Eliot follows a representative line of English poet-critics. And often, in Eliot, we see the intellect which makes him so admirable a critic presiding over his poetry. The poetic passion, the intense moment of creation is filtered through a complex verbal wall and dressed in metaphors which flow from the mind. Neither James nor Eliot is capable of taking the reader on a journey into the blackness of the night; if they brilliantly examine what the darkness has meant, they do so in broad daylight. We do not always experience their passion: but we look upon it through the illumination of their intellect and their civilization—and by this process are led to new experience.

In their experiments with form they stand on common ground, both as artists and as Americans. Their strong sense of "craft" may be discerned as a national trait, as artist-products of a civilization concerned with the highest skills and the greatest efficiencies. As James was the exponent of "point of view" in the novel, so Eliot has espoused it consistently in poetry. It is a method essentially dramatic and it stems, originally, from the monologues of Browning, which influenced both the American novelist and the American poet. What Eliot has done has been simply to move the thoughts of his speaker more deeply into the consciousness; the monologue—understandably in the era of Joyce—is more "inner" than it was in the time of James and Browning. I have already referred to Eliot's illuminating lecture on *The Three Voices of Poetry* in which he explains that when we read a poem we hear the voice of the poet talking to himself; or again, the voice may be addressing an audience; or (and this would be the third voice), the poet may speak through a character of his own creation, or in the guise of some figure out of the past. But always we hear the voice of the poet and it is not a disembodied voice. This very formulation reveals to us Eliot's sense of poetry as drama, and as embodying within it the dynamism of the audible as well as the visual. The voice we hear in the theater is always the third voice, that of characters imagined by the dramatist, acting themselves out in words before our eyes. They live for us in what they say and what they reveal of themselves. But in the process they also reveal their creator.

The poet speaking to himself, the poet addressing an audience in his own voice, or in an assumed one—what are these if not the voices of soliloquy and the chorus of the ancient and modern stage? In our century, however, precisely through the understanding of *point of view*, we have penetrated more deeply into the inner modes and the inner life of these voices, so that sometimes we are brought closer to the actual flow of thought in the speaker. His "stream of consciousness," or "inner monologue," translated into verbal images or symbols, places us, the readers or listeners, close to the actual emotional experience of the character—and the author. The words and the images, the symbols they place before us (in Eliot's complex statement of this complex creative process) are the *objective correlative* of the emotional state of the creator, as a shadow is a projection of an image of the body. Helen Gardner, in her study of Eliot's art, gives us an illuminating example of the process by quoting a passage from the poet's prose and showing us the manner in which the same data was used by him in his poetry. The prose passage is to be found in Eliot's essay on *The Use of Poetry.* He is speaking of the poet's imagery and he says:

It comes from the whole of his sensitive life since

early childhood. Why, for all of us, out of all that we have heard, seen, felt, in a lifetime, do certain images recur, charged with emotion, rather than others? The song of one bird, the leap of one fish, at a particular place and time, the scent of one flower, an old woman on a German mountain path, six ruffians seen through an open window playing cards at night at a small French railway junction where there was a water-mill; such memories may have symbolic value, but of what we cannot tell, for they come to represent depths of feeling into which we cannot peer.

That we can sometimes peer into these depths Proust has shown. But what is significant for us is that this "felt life," as James called it, without necessarily being analyzed, makes its way into artistic utterance. Let us see how the third voice of poetry—the voice of an old man in the *Journey of the Magi*—takes these items of Eliot's experience into the realm of general symbolic experience:

> Then at dawn we came down to a temperate valley,
> Wet, below the snow line, smelling of vegetation;
> With a running stream and a water-mill beating the darkness,
> And three trees on the low sky,
> And an old white horse galloped away in the meadow.
> Then we came to a tavern with vine-leaves over the lintel,
> Six hands at an open door dicing for pieces of silver,
> And feet kicking the empty wine-skins.

Here the old personal memories of Eliot have melted together with older memories of the history of man and of Calvary, the three trees, the six hands dicing for silver, the blood-wine.

Eliot places us usually within the dramatized thoughts and reflections of himself as poet, or those he has imparted to his created character, whether it be Prufrock, the aged narrator in the *Magi*, or the lady of his *Portrait of a Lady*. And this becomes one of the difficulties we experience in reading him, for we must recognize for ourselves the particular voice that addresses us and then try to capture from the sequence of images the quality and the emotion of the utterance. A further difficulty is created by Eliot's discreet borrowing of lines and phrases from literature, past and present. Such depth of allusion is an endless source of fascination for explicators and footnote writers (whom Eliot seems to have partly emulated and partly mocked in his notes to *The Waste Land*), but it tends to confuse the reader accustomed to the old lucidities and simplicities of lyric and dramatic poetry. He may experience a slight irritation when he discovers that a certain line he has admired is not in reality Eliot, but Spenser or Shakespeare, or is taken from some obscure long-ago sermon. Such irritation may be overcome— and is certainly groundless—if we recognize how often in our daily speech we ourselves use phrases out of the past, from the Bible, or the Declaration of Independence, or books or poems read and reread, without its ever occurring to us that we must acknowledge these borrowings; often, indeed, we have forgotten that we are quoting someone else. Verbal experience, like all experience, is a constant composite of old and new, and when Eliot records memories of things he has read, which become a part of *his* experience of the moment, he is concerned not with the source of this or that quotation he may be using, but with the emotion which the line or lines may contain for him. These lines are so many possessions of his own consciousness, or of the character he has adumbrated and made to speak to us in the poem.

We must see Eliot's poetry, therefore, as part of a complex projection into words, not only of the poet's meditations but of actual states of consciousness, some seemingly inchoate, some as organized as the old-fashioned soliloquies. And these attempts to capture the "lifetime burning in every moment" open for the biographer fascinating apertures into Mr. Eliot's life. "In some minds," he once said, "certain memories, both from reading and from life, become charged with emotional significance. All these are used, so that intensity is gained at the expense of clarity."

What is gained is an intense vision of the poet's experience, and this prompts me to set myself a small exercise in biographical empiricism. So far I have been making general observations on the characteristics revealed when we broadly survey Mr. Eliot's work. Let us now look into certain of the poems and try to read them for what they will reveal of the face behind the mask. We can hardly attempt, in this small compass, an exhaustive "inner" reading of the entire work, which would yield us the best portrait. But a few representative poems, taken in sequence, should suggest to us some of the "emotional significance" to which Eliot alludes.

VII

We are in the happy position, for this experiment, of having no access to the poet's private life. There are no letters, save those published by Mr. Eliot himself, largely letters to editors on literary questions which show him as a writer *engagé* in the world of his time. Two volumes containing appreciative essays have also been published containing, I can see as I turn their pages, some biographical odds and ends. But I turn the pages hastily and resist the temptation to read them at this time. I have not even read Mr. Eliot's entry in Who's Who and am therefore in that blissful state of biographical ignorance to which every "new critic" fondly aspires. I have read, with much profit, long ago, F. O. Matthiessen's critical book on the poet; and more recently Helen Gardner's admirable critical study. It is true that in one of Mr. Eliot's French poems I find certain lines which may be autobiographical: these speak of being a professor in America, a journalist in England, a lecturer in Yorkshire, a "bit of" a bohemian in London and in Paris, one of those individuals—we translate a little freely—who "didn't give a damn." But such biographical details, if accurate, hardly represent the "hidden life" which we want to find in the work; they belong to another area of biography.

It may be useful at this point to elucidate my method. In seeking the inner emotion of Mr. Eliot's poetry I start fairly obviously with the axiom that the poem is the poet's and no one else's; the words, the structure, the poem's character and psychology issue from the poet's inner consciousness; its contents are tissued out of those memories of reading and of life that have become emotionally charged. In saying this we reject the old and rather naïve concept of the happy artistic inspiration which just "flew" *into* the poet's mind. The flight is outward, from assimilated experience. We predicate, in this process, a series of choices open to the artist. Thus Mr. Eliot chose to imagine J. Alfred Prufrock; he selected the particular mirthful and yet sad-sounding name. He might have imagined someone like Bishop Blougram or Rabbi Ben Ezra or the articulate Italian painters whose monologues speak to us from the pages of Robert Browning. Instead we listen to the monologue of a melancholy middle-aged man who somehow can't assert himself, not even in his imagination when he thinks of conversing with mermaids. The creation of the person of Prufrock, however mythical a figure, is thus a reflection of a certain *state of feeling* within the poet at the time the poem was written. Moreover, having the world's literature from which to choose, Mr. Eliot has placed as epigraph to the poem a passage from Dante which gives us, we find, the poem's theme. Doubtless this is one of the "memories from reading" of which Mr. Eliot spoke. The *persona* of Prufrock, and the poet's theme, constitute a mask selected from many possible masks.

Let us try to remove the mask by a careful reading of this poem, which is characteristic of Eliot's early work. His first poems mock polite society and the tea hound or "cookie-pusher," the man who has measured out his life with coffee spoons, while at the same time being aware of his feeling of impotence and his frustrated strivings. The petty conformities of the drawing room, symbol of an ordered and vacuous world, are invoked; already the poet is smiling at his hostesses while he murders them with a phrase or a thought; and Prufrock, wandering on the beach, finds his buried feelings and deeper intensities expressed in the surging waves, the breaking foam. He is hardly a Hamlet; but he possesses Hamlet's inner melancholy, and his indecision. The voice of the poet, speaking to us in the guise of Prufrock, is that of an individual who has depths of feeling which have been tamed and cultivated and disciplined, and therefore have never been fully expressed. Reticence, gentility, petty conformity have smothered emotion; the poet assumes the guise of the disillusioned middle-aged who have found little meaning in life and wonder whether "it has been worth while after all."

As with most of Eliot's poems, we must pay close attention to the epigraph, for it carries in it an overtone of the work, some association in the poet's mind linked, as we saw, to the center of his feeling. In this case he has chosen certain lines from Dante, a passage from Canto XXVII of the *Inferno*. The speaker is Guido da Montefeltro, reduced in hell to a hovering flame because he gave false counsel. He tells Dante in these lines that if he believed he were answering the questions of someone returning to earth (as Dante was supposed to return), he would be at rest. But since he is sure that there is no turning back from hell for anyone, he can speak without fear of infamy. In the rest of the canto he tells Dante about his life as a deceiver, how his needs were those of the sly fox rather than of a bold lion. If we search the inner meaning of the passage in Dante and the substance of *Prufrock*, we see that Eliot also has written a poem about false counsel. A man, J. Alfred Prufrock has bowed and smirked, put on a face other than his own, done what he was supposed to do socially, instead of yielding to his own natural feelings. Moreover, he dares not depart from this role. He is afraid: and has been afraid, afraid even to speak his love to women. He longs to be daring; to walk along the beach in carefree fashion and in informal attire; to talk boldly to mermaids; but if he did, he is sure they would not reply. He has become a middle-aged Little Lord Fauntleroy: the fear of self-assertion is combined with the fear that he might meet rebuff. All this makes him see himself as rather a fool, a jester in life.

Like Guido, who deceived and tried to conform to other people's values, he has ended by playing a rather frightful trick on himself. For in being untrue to oneself one ends by being untrue to others. The "love song" of Mr. Prufrock is ironic; being incapable of any love but self-love, and facing the world with a mask of deceit, he must sing his love song, so to speak, to himself.

Mr. Sweeney of "Sweeney Among the Nightingales" is rather more robust than J. Alfred Prufrock and compulsive in quite a different way. There is something of the orangutan about him, as we are told. One thinks of him as measuring out his life with jiggers of whiskey rather than with coffee spoons. The quatrains which celebrate Sweeney's little melodrama have set their stamp upon modern poetry with their verbal-visual sharpness, their *hardness* of statement, and their pulsing beat. Lively and witty and dramatic as this poem is, it contains within it deeper despair than is revealed in *Prufrock*. Again the epigraph attracts our attention. It is in Greek and it can be translated "Alas, I am struck a mortal blow within"—the climactic cry of the betrayed Agamemnon in the tragedy by Aeschylus. The effect is ironic: a memory of high tragedy is invoked for a tale of a thick-necked individual named Sweeney, threatened by death in some gangster dive. To the nightingales—as to the worms in Hamlet—this is a matter of complete indifference. The nightingales will sing alike for king or gangster; as a consequence of the industry of worms, a king may make a progress through the guts of a beggar. The exquisite music of the nightingales sounded when the mortal blow was struck in ancient Greece; and they sing while Sweeney is under the eye of the man in mocha brown and has his little adventure with the intoxicated night-town lady in the Spanish cape. Eliot has been quoted as saying that he is aware only of having tried to create in his poem a "sense of foreboding." But the effect, up to the last two stanzas, is rather that of movie melodrama and comedy. Then the mood changes: the poet is suddenly solemn, meditative, philosophical. He muses on the fact that the deaths of a king and of a man named Sweeney are of equal importance, (even if one is a tragic hero and the other is apelike and commonplace). Beauty and ugliness are juxtaposed, the tragic emotion and the pathetic; and the nightingales offer a requiem of indifference to one or the other, much as the droppings of the birds are indifferent to the shroud that decks the remains of a king.

These moods of boredom, futility, despair and sterility—reach climactic utterance in *The Waste Land,* which Eliot published in 1922 (the year of Joyce's *Ulysses*). In this poem life and history are seen as drained of all fertility; there has been a monstrous dehydration of the land and of the soul; the world is drab, uniform, mechanized. Questions are asked for which there are no answers:

> Do
> You know nothing? Do you see nothing? Do you remember
> Nothing?

Or if there is an answer, it is death:

> I remember
> Those are pearls that were his eyes.

Once again we must scrutinize the epigraph. In this case Eliot is quoting Petronius, and the Greek words, set into the Latin, are question and response: "With my own eyes I saw the Sybil at Cumae hanging in a bottle, and when the lads said to her: *Sybil, what do you want?* she would answer: *I want to die.*"

Thus if we consider Eliot's poetry in sequence the frustration and impotence and the boredom of the earlier poems, and the foreboding of Sweeney, have become despair and yearning for death. The waste land is that inner drying up of the will to live, because life has lost its meaning and the pain of existence craves the anaesthesia of death. But if the yearning for death is self-destructive and a negation of life, the desire to escape from the waste land can carry in it an affirmation of life as well: it is that affirmation which Hamlet voices when, in his great soliloquy, he fears eternal sleep in case it may be disrupted by dream. So the poet in the waste land, his senses numbed by the drying up of life, finds that they are still capable of responding to all that is fertile and beautiful and waste-defeating. There is not yet that deadly apathy and emptiness of despair which could turn the wish for death into an act of self-annihilation. The eyes that look upon the desert land know also that what has been lost may be recovered.

If we allow some such emotions as constituting the deepest sources of this poem—and we take our cue for them from the epigraph—we can then reread the work, keeping in mind always Eliot's formulation of the *objective correlative,* and see in the images and symbols projected by the poet the concretions into which the emotions have been translated. To search out the meaning of the poem by annotating it even beyond the annotations of Mr. Eliot is perhaps a pleasant intellectual exercise, and on occasion a scholarly necessity, but the way to the heart of *The Waste Land* lies elsewhere. For the reader concerned with the poem's essence it is more profitable to see how the image of a waste land, the central image, is translated into its multiple forms and into its antithesis. If, on the one hand, we are in a desert world of heat and dryness, shadowless life, empty cisterns and decayed cities, we are also led to reflect on opposites: the return of the seasons, the freshness of the water, the age-old vegetation and fertility myths, the rituals surrounding birth and growth, life and death, and the relation of the cycles of life to a divine order.

The reader who is willing to accept Eliot's sacrifice of lucidity for intensity, and to treat the poem not as a test of memory or an elaborate literary puzzle, may not grasp all that he will read and yet be capable of capturing the force and beauty of the language and the poetic pictures—and emotions—evoked. The poem is a series of visions, narrative moments expressed in lyric and dramatic terms. We begin with the round of the seasons, old memories, the fortuneteller; we move into a Prufrockian London ("Unreal City"); we listen to a conversation in a pub; we meditate Hamlet-like with the poet; or see with the aid of the blind seer Tiresias such episodes as that of the tired typist and her carbuncular young man and their love-making, as automatic as their gramophone. The Thames flows sweetly through the poem with its unsweet burden and its historic memories; and the poet, standing in London, possesses the historic memory of Carthage, burning and leveled to waste land. (Years later this will seem almost prophetic when the poet will actually see London ablaze during the Second World War.) If fire consumes, so can water. Phlebas the Phoenician has been drowned, and Eliot's lyric recounts this in a kind of water music. And then the voice of Thunder, the emanation of the unknown and the final images of desiccation and death, the deserts of the world and the soul, but the hope also for rain and for eternal calm.

That *The Waste Land* possessed much meaning for its readers is clear, for it was read by many—and for years—without benefit of explication. And if we listen to Eliot's "three voices of poetry" in it, we can figure the poem as a discovery of the dark wood into which the poet has wandered in the middle of the journey. The poet is descending into the abyss.

Continuing our reading of certain of Eliot's works (always in sequence so that we may capture, if possible, the emotional continuum), we come upon *The Hollow Men*. The title itself arrests us. It follows immediately upon *The Waste Land* and is of 1925. On this occasion we must examine two epigraphs. "Mistah Kurtz—he dead" is the ominous climax of Joseph Conrad's *Heart of Darkness,* the tale of a dark journey into the jungle and a no less dark and awesome journey into the depths of the self, those depths of the unconscious which Kurtz reached when he espoused the savagery of the jungle. The second epigraph, "A penny for the Old Guy," alludes to another figure associated with violence, the Guy Fawkes of English history, whose gunpowder plot was foiled and who to this day is burned in effigy. In the poem itself there are allusions to Dante—to death's other kingdom and death's dream kingdom. The heart of darkness is also the bottom of hell; and the bottom of hell is also the bottom of one's own despair. The very imagery of this poem suggests that the poet has reached the heart of his darkness:

> Shape without form, shade without colour,
> Paralysed force, gesture without motion;

The Waste Land has in it the awareness of its sterility; its images of dryness and the fear embodied in dust still partake of life. But the "waste land" of *The Hollow Men* is waste indeed. It is the soul's emptiness when life has lost its last shred of meaning; the hollow men stuffed with straw are scarecrows in vague human shape. What we have in reality is complete dehumanization. The swinging tree, the broken column, the stone images, the broken jaw of some animal become the metaphor for a lost kingdom, "this last of meeting places" by the river, where the shades in Dante wait to be ferried into the regions from which there is no return. The indifference of death and the indifference of the nightingales are all one. There is no longer even a yearning to die: there is emptiness and a babble of the fragments of the Lord's Prayer mingled with nursery rhyme and

> the world ends
> Not with a bang but a whimper.

Ash Wednesday, which came five years after *The Hollow Men,* marks the ascent from the nether regions, the long climb, as it were, through purgatory. The poet,

85

speaking in his first or second voice to himself and to an audience, seems to be looking for some center of peace; he seeks his salvation; he has set foot outside the dryness of waste land, away from the miasma of the heart of darkness. As its title suggests, *Ash Wednesday* is a deeply religious poem. The voice speaking to us has embraced Christianity and is coming to terms with past and present, "for what is done . . . May the judgement not be too heavy upon us." The poet rejoices, "having to construct something/Upon which to rejoice." The symbolism of this poem is intricate and derives from religious ritual and religious meditation. There are ambiguities of feeling and uncertainties, doubts, and indecisions. The lines are as of the chants and responses, the incantations and reiterations of the religious service. By writing such a poem the poet shows he is ready for peace, as Dante was for the *Paradiso*. He can move forward toward that repose of the heart which comes from the knowledge of agitation surmounted, tranquillity experienced.

We find this in *Four Quartets* (1940–42) in which Eliot summed up the twenty years of his middle life, between the two World Wars. We have moved now from the early disguises, the *personae* assumed by the poet, to something that comes closer to autobiography, fragments out of the poet's continuum of experience, but experience now brought to the level of self-analysis and intellectual appraisal. "To make an end is to make a beginning"—and the terminal point of *The Hollow Men*, the bottom of the pit, was followed by an ascent from these nether regions. We hear the poet in the act of meditation—on time, on history, on feeling, on the poet's craft. Or he is candidly reminiscential

So here I am, in the middle way, having had twenty
years—
Twenty years largely wasted, the years of *l'entre
deux guerres*—
Trying to learn to use words, and every attempt
Is a wholly new start, and a different kind of failure

And so he finds that history is "a pattern of timeless moments," and the poet's craft makes him spokesman for
the moment:

For last year's words belong to last year's language
And next year's words await another voice.

For most men there is "only the unattended/Moment,
the moment in and out of time." For the rest, there
is "prayer, observance, discipline, thought and action."
The quartets are compounded of the visual and the
dramatic; by a series of subtle devices Eliot expresses,
in the loftiest and also the most delicately shaded
phrasings, his deep sense of man's inner tumult and
the calm that awaits him through sentience, expression
of feeling, as in prayer, self-acceptance, and acceptance of Christian love—

Love is most nearly itself
When here and now cease to matter.

But to sum up in this fashion certain of the ideas in
the quartets does not suggest their intricacy of pattern
and nuance of thought. The critics have seen that each
quartet deals with one of the four elements: *East Coker*
with earth, *Burnt Norton* with air, *The Dry Salvages*
with water, and *Little Gidding* with fire. The air raids
on London brought fire and water together; but water
is also baptism, and fire purges—and water (as in *The*

Waste Land) betokens fertility while fire is a destroyer as well as a renewer of life. Thus Eliot sounds the universal symbols and the eternal ambiguities. The quartets are of a piece with *The Waste Land,* but in them the search and the questioning are over. The poet has discovered his answers. He now knows repose and the largeness of serenity.

Our little experiment with the poems of T. S. Eliot demonstrates the way in which literary work can yield biography; if we were to search Eliot's essays and plays, we would find more material of a similar sort; not only the poems but the entire work can be said to be the *objective correlative* to the inner life of T. S. Eliot. The works, in other words, are palpable projections of the impalpable and wholly personal inner experience. The poems have their own completeness, inevitably; part of their function has been to depersonalize the deeply felt feelings; they thus become independent works of art which, in their totality, harbor within them the autobiography of the psyche. The actual facts of Mr. Eliot's ordeal—the plunge from early clever Prufrockian intellectuality into self-disparagement and the depths of despair—which a biographer might seek to discover, may be relevant for the study of the creative process; they might show us *how* the poet transformed his deepest experience into disciplined art. But I hold it to be clear that by the very act of criticism the "invulnerable granite" can yield that part of the writer which is most important to literary biography—more important than any accumulation of external detail or any bundle of "sources" and "influences" out of the poet's education and reading.

If we are thus led from the work to the man, from the mask to the face and to the mind and consciousness, it follows that in modern biography we are led by the same avenue to that study which has brought to our generation a greater understanding of the mind and the human consciousness. The literary biographer must be a literary critic; and as a critic he must come to terms with certain other disciplines explaining man, and particularly—in our century—psychoanalysis. What shall the biographer do with the new psychology? How is he to make use of these glittering twentieth-century tools offered to him by Sigmund Freud and his disciples and the other schools of psychoanalysis which have come in Freud's wake? This question warrants further pursuit.

IV Psychoanalysis

I

In these discourses I have tried to suggest that modern biography—and in particular the biography of imaginative writers—has undergone a marked development in our century. From the undocumented life, speculatively erected around a few meager facts, more straw than bricks, we have come to the life of documentary surfeit, and the biographer has had to learn how to keep from putting up biographical skyscrapers. I have shown how his quest has been altered as a result of man's growing consciousness of himself as a figure in a continuum of history, and the strange and even macabre duel that can occur between subject and biographer—a matching of wits in an unequal battle between the dead and the living. We have looked into the relations between biography and criticism and seen that the biographer is committed at every turn to the act of criticism. And now I should like to examine the newest and most significant of all the biographer's relationships: his as yet uneasy flirtation with psychology.

It would be somewhat more accurate to speak of it as psychoanalysis rather than psychology, formidable and forbidding though that sounds. Psychology is the study

of human behavior: it is an all-inclusive term. Psychoanalysis is the term applied to the special techniques
developed by Sigmund Freud and elaborated by his
successors for the study of the symbols evoked by man
which can explain his behavior. Neither term is altogether satisfactory for our purposes; the one is too
large and the other too narrow. In the psychoanalytic
process the analyst has constant access to the symbol
life of his subject—dreams; modes of expression (such
as slips of the tongue and the pen); association; the
interconnections of experience; rationalization; involuntary memory; the events of everyday life. A biographer also deals in such materials: they are the ones
I have pictured to you as cluttering his large table. But
what a difference there is between having such inert
data on a desk and having the subject in front of you
in a chair or on a couch! A biographer can never, in
reality, psychoanalyze his documents; and yet he is
concerned with the same kinds of symbols as the
psychoanalyst.

The many confusions and misunderstandings which
arise between literature and psychology begin in the
fact that psychoanalysts have found—as Freud did
from the beginning—that the life of the imagination,
and especially of great figures in literature, is highly
illustrative. When they look for archetypes or univer-
sals they discover them in such figures as Oedipus or
Hamlet. The result is that they venture frequently
upon literary ground and sometimes indeed into places
where angels fear to tread, leaving (from the point of
view of the student of literature) large, muddy footprints in their wake. Possessing neither the discipline
of criticism nor the methods of biography, they import
the atmosphere of the clinic and the consulting room

into the library. And what they write is not, in reality, so much a contribution to the study of literature—I do not believe they make any such extravagant claim—but an illustration of this or that aspect of their own technical work.

The other side of the picture has been, inevitably, the venture on the part of critics and biographers upon psychoanalytic ground, where they have been no less inexpert than the psychoanalysts on *our* ground. The use of the psychoanalytic tool involves high skills, some quasi-scientific; a deep saturation in the problems of the mind and of the emotions; and a grasp of certain phenomena—such as "projection" or "distortion" or "malevolent transformation." We have thus a common problem: that of certain individuals who are perfectly competent in their proper field but who seem prepared to blazon forth their incompetence on ground where they do not belong.

It is not difficult to understand therefore that there has been, in the academy, a vigorous resistance to "psychologizing" and a tendency to stop up one's ears the moment a psychoanalyst arrives on the scene and tries to explain that what was wrong with Robert Louis Stevenson was that he had a feeding problem; that having as an infant been denied his mother's breast he sought ever after to gratify his oral needs—which was why he dreamed up *Dr. Jekyll and Mr. Hyde* and hinged the story on the swallowing of a potion, or why he could hold his own so splendidly at the prodigious daylong feasts in Hawaii and Samoa. This, they further tell us, meant that he never really became a mature adult. It so happens that they are not entirely wrong. Mrs. Stevenson kept a diary when Louis was an infant; and certain of his problems could be traced in psychoanalytic terms to his infantile difficulties there recorded. But isn't the important thing in all this *not* that Stevenson, for deep reasons about which we can only speculate, retained certain childish elements in his make-up—but that out of these grew the eternally youthful *Treasure Island?* And if there was this duality within him, how admirably equipped he was to trace the double sides of man's nature, as he did in the story of Jekyll and his hideous counterpart! In a word, the process of applying psychoanalysis to literature in a purely diagnostic sense invariably ends up by reducing the artist to a neurosis. Perhaps the artist *was* "neurotic." We are interested, however, in how he not only triumphs over his wound, but acquires, because of it, a kind of second sight. I need not go here into the whole troubled question of art and neurosis, which would take us far afield. Mr. Lionel Trilling has written one of his most measured essays on this subject and we have had Edmund Wilson's book *The Wound and the Bow* before us for almost two decades. The literature is large and important. Indeed, Charles Lamb, as Mr. Trilling reminds us, wrote a penetrating essay "On the Sanity of True Genius" long before the advent of psychoanalysis. Men, Lamb observed, "finding in the raptures of the higher poetry a condition of exaltation, to which they have no parallel in their own experience, besides the spurious resemblance of it in dreams and fevers, impute a state of dreaminess and fever to the poet. But the true poet dreams being awake. He is not possessed by his subject but has dominion over it. . . . Where he seems most to recede from humanity, he will be found the truest to it."

Art is the result not of calm and tranquillity, however much the artist may, on occasion, experience calm in the act of writing. It springs from tension and passion, from a state of disequilibrium in the artist's being. "His art is happy, but who knows his mind?" William Butler Yeats asked in speaking of Keats. The psychoanalyst, reading the pattern of the work, can attempt to tell us what was wrong with the artist's mental or psychic health. The biographer, reading the same pattern in the larger picture of the human condition, seeks to show how the negatives were converted into positives: how Proust translated his allergies and his withdrawal from the pain of experience, into the whole world of Combray, capturing in language the very essences which seemed illusory and evanescent in man's consciousness; how Virginia Woolf, on the margin of her melancholy, pinned the feeling of the moment to the printed page as the hunter of butterflies pins his diaphanous and fluttering prize to his; and how James Joyce, visioning himself as Daedalus soaring over a world he had mastered, created a language for it, the word-salads of *Finnegans Wake*—but where the schizophrenic patient creates word-salads because of his madness, Joyce created them with that method in madness which Lamb was describing when he spoke of the artist's dominion over his subject. These are the triumphs of art over neurosis, and of literature over life, as I have had occasion to say elsewhere, and they illustrate Henry James's assertion to H. G. Wells that "it is art that *makes* life, makes interest, makes importance . . . and I know of no substitute whatever for the force and beauty of its process."

In one supreme instance in recent times, the psychoanalyst and the biographer have become one. I refer to Dr. Ernest Jones and the three substantial volumes in which he recorded the life of Sigmund Freud. Dr.

Jones wrote out of a deep friendship and a Boswellian knowledge of his subject's life; he wrote also from extensive documents made available to him by the Freud family and as a disciple who had himself arrived at a mastery of psychoanalysis. He ran the inevitable biographical risk of apotheosizing his dead leader; but having himself been analyzed he could say at the outset (as he did) that "my own hero-worshipping propensities had been worked through before I encountered [Freud]." Dr. Jones had fewer difficulties in his quest for data than many biographers, although Freud, like Henry James, leveled the approaches to certain areas of his early life by destruction of personal papers. The remaining mass was considerable, however, and more important still, there was available to Dr. Jones in Freud's voluminous writings—the writings of a man with a profound literary sense—much of his subject's self-exploration and his dream life.

The result was a biography of major scope as befitted the luminous mind it celebrated; and a work which uses psychoanalysis constantly while being in itself a partial history of psychoanalysis. *The Life and Work of Sigmund Freud* will probably stand as an archetypal study, illustrating the relation of psychoanalysis to biography—and in negative as well as positive ways. Its shortcomings, for the literary biographer, are fairly obvious: they reside in Dr. Jones's ready use of that language—the concepts, assumptions, conclusions—to which he was accustomed and which had become second nature to him, but which is confusing to the uninitiated reader. The reader without psychoanalytic orientation is asked to make too many leaps and to hurdle ideas that by everyday standards appear strange and inconsistent, and indeed are still open to debate within the psychoanalytic disciplines. One example will suffice. In the first chapter Dr. Jones describes the emotional problems which beset the two-year-old Freud upon the impending birth of another child in the family:

> Darker problems arose when it dawned on him that some man was even more intimate with his mother than he was. Before he was two years old, for the second time another baby was on the way, and soon visibly so. Jealousy of the intruder, and anger for whoever had seduced his mother into such an unfaithful proceeding, were inevitable. Discarding his knowledge of the sleeping conditions in the house, he rejected the unbearable thought that the nefarious person could be his beloved and perfect father.

One needs to be more than merely conversant with Freudian theory to grasp this picture of a childish consciousness told in the terms of adult sexuality. Dr. Jones was inevitably much less concerned with the *translation* of his specialized concepts into the language of everyday life. The literary biographer, when he borrows the psychoanalyst's code, is obliged to decipher it and render it into the language proper to literature and literary discussion.

II

Literature and psychology are not necessarily antagonistic, as they have been made to seem. They meet on common ground. We have for decades used psychology in criticism and in biography. When we study the motivations of Hamlet, is not this psychology? When we try to understand and speculate upon symbols in a work, are we not "psychologizing"? And in our time, when creative writers have been exposed directly to the works of Freud and Jung and their disciples and use them in their writings, we must treat them for the sources that they are. How can we understand William Faulkner's *Light in August* without at least a glance at certain modern theories of "conditioning" and behavior? Can we deal adequately with *Finnegans Wake* without looking into Jung and his theory of the collective unconscious? What meaning can Eugene O'Neill's *Strange Interlude* and *Mourning Becomes Electra* have if they are divorced from the popular Freudian misconceptions of the 1920's? Freud himself acknowledged that Sophocles and Dostoevsky and Ibsen had those glimpses into the unconscious which were vouchsafed to him in his consulting room. The answer to the misguided use of psychoanalysis is not to close our ears, but to ask ourselves: how are we to handle this difficult material while remaining true to our own disciplines—and avoid making complete fools of ourselves?

Well, it is fairly obvious that we can handle it only after we have studied and mastered that part of psychology useful to us, as we must master any learning. Our success will depend entirely on the extent to which we know what we are about and the way in which we learn to use this new and intricate code. We must not run amuck; above all we must beware of the terminology and jargon of the psychoanalysts. What we must try to do is to translate the terms in a meaningful way and into language proper to our discipline. Critics who babble of the Oedipus complex and who plant psychoanalytical clichés higgledy-piggledy in their writings do a disservice both to literature and to psychoanalysis.

Biographers who take certain arbitrary symbols and apply them rigidly to the wholly volatile human personality, inevitably arrive at gross and ludicrous distortions. These are matters highly complex and difficult to explain, and I have accordingly devised an illustrative problem in an effort to demonstrate what I would deem to be the use—and the abuse—of psychoanalysis in the writing of biography.

I intend to draw upon certain material presented in the Alexander Lectures of 1949–50 in E. K. Brown's discussion of *Rhythm in the Novel.* I am going to take that portion of the third lecture in which Brown discussed Willa Cather's novel *The Professor's House,* a passage later incorporated into his biography of Miss Cather. The passage in question shows Brown at his best as critic and explicator; he evokes the central symbol of the novel—the house—and illuminates it wholly in the light of his own critical intelligence. I will then try, as fairly as I can, to show how the psychoanalyst would handle this same material in a broad diagnostic sense; and finally I will try to show how the biographer, using the material offered by the critic and the psychoanalyst, can more deeply illuminate the work by seeking to determine what the house symbol meant to Miss Cather herself. First, however, let us look at the story.

III

The Professor's House, published in September 1925, is the story of a professor in a Midwestern university who has achieved success but derives no particular pleasure from it. The novel is a record of his mental depression. With the money received from a prize he has won for a monumental historical work, Professor

St. Peter has built a new house to please his wife and daughters. He would prefer to remain in the rented house in which he has shaped his career for thirty years. Indeed he cannot bring himself to move out of his old study, located in the attic, where still stand the wire forms on which a dressmaker fitted the clothes for his wife and growing daughters. The attic sewing room is lit by an oil lamp. It is heated by a stove. Professor St. Peter has scorned cushion comforts. He had a "show" study downstairs and has one in the new house. But the attic room, with its silent dummies, is comfort enough for him. He clings to the old place even after the rest of the house has been emptied and the moving is over. Since the lease still has some months to run, he decides he will keep his former workroom until he has to give it up.

His elder daughter is Rosamond, an attractive girl who has married a suave, fast-talking, pretentious but cultivated young man named Louie Marsellus. Marsellus has, with great practicality, turned to commercial use in aviation a certain discovery made by one of the professor's former students, Tom Outland, who was Rosamond's fiancé but who was killed during the First World War. Outland bequeathed his patent to Rosamond, and since her marriage to Marsellus it has become a source of wealth. The professor loves his daughter very much, but intensely dislikes the upstart qualities of her husband, and accordingly feels a certain alienation from her. The professor's wife, however, is extremely fond of her son-in-law and his European affectations. She feels that her husband, in his withdrawal from the entire family, does not sufficiently recognize how materially its fortunes are being altered by Louie Marsellus's business acumen. There is a second daughter who is married to a newspaper columnist named McGregor. They tend to side with the father against the somewhat vulgar *nouveau riche* world of Louie and Rosamond. The latter are also building a house—in the style of a Norwegian manor, set incongruously in this Midwestern community.

The first part of the book, titled "The Family," sketches for us the professor's alienation from those closest to him because of his feeling that his wife and daughters do not really understand his deeper emotional life, and his rebellion against the crass materialism of the college town. He has set himself apart rather successfully over the years. He has made for himself a French garden in this prairie setting; he has cultivated his love for French wines and delicate sauces; he has a beach house on the lake and spends long lonely hours in the water. He is a Gallic epicure isolated, like his garden, in surroundings to which he cannot ever wholly belong. He has had only one student in all the years of his teaching who has meant anything to him— Tom Outland. He dislikes the new generation of students. He dislikes college politics. He has no real friends among his colleagues. He feels himself oppressed by the prosaic, mediocre world of the town of which his wife and daughters are so much a part. Material values have been exalted here over those he cherishes: the rich fabric of art related to the rich fabric of the old religion in which great cathedrals and the drama of Good and Evil exalted men to a high creativity.

The second part of the book is called "Tom Outland's Story." Here Miss Cather attempts a risky technical device, which is nevertheless time-honored in fiction. In the manner of Cervantes or Smollett she interpolates a story within a story: she gives us an autobiographical fragment written by Tom Outland and confided to Professor St. Peter. It describes a crucial episode in the young man's life. Miss Cather explained that in writing this part of the novel she had in mind those Dutch paintings in which interiors are scrupulously rendered; in many of these there was "a square window, open, through which one saw the masts of ships, or a stretch of gray sea"; the effect is that of an inset, a picture within a picture. Having given us the interior of the professor's family life, she directs our attention to the one important window in it—the one that looks out upon Tom Outland's adventure.

The crucial episode had been his discovery of a Cliff Dwellers' village tucked into a wall of rock high in a New Mexico canyon. Here was beauty at once primitive and sophisticated. Here were houses that let in wind and sun and yet sheltered an unfathomable past. Here also was a great tower: "It was still as sculpture. . . . The tower was the fine thing that held all the jumble of houses together and made them mean something. . . . That village sat looking down into the cañon with the calmness of eternity." The Cliff Dwellers' houses are never overtly contrasted with the houses in the professor's town, but they invite contrast. In the modern town the emphasis, as E. K. Brown observes, is on the individual buildings. In the ancient village it is on the architectural as well as the social unity.

Tom made his discovery with the aid of a fellow cowpuncher, Roddy. He traveled to Washington in great excitement to inform the Department of the Interior, bringing with him samples of the ancient pottery he had found in the long-deserted houses. In the capital he is promptly wrapped up in heedless red tape; he sits in impersonal outer offices; he is met with general indifference. Civil servants seem to him strange modern cave dwellers living in rows of apartments as if in rabbit warrens; and their careerism and arrogance blot out all his hopes. He turns his back on Washington, disillusioned; he had felt he had done the proper thing as a citizen, but the petty officials did not share his interest in his country's distant past. However, a still greater disappointment awaited him. Roddy, during his prolonged absence, had profited by the arrival of a German anthropologist to sell the entire contents of the cliff town. The ancient relics had been packed and shipped to Europe, and Roddy had deposited the money for Tom in a bank thinking he had driven a good bargain. Tom, in anger at what he considered a betrayal, broke with Roddy and then returned to the cliff town to spend a few days in magnificent solitude, hiding in the high tower his notes and records of the entire adventure. Then, descending again, he withdrew the money from the bank and used it to go to college, there meeting the professor who became his guide and mentor.

The final part of the novel is a mere sketch. Titled "The Professor," it returns to the dilemma of St. Peter's isolation in his attic. Lonely and depressed, he remains there while his family is away during the summer, living a monastic dream life, with the old sewing woman turning up to act as charwoman. One day, on awakening from a nap, he discovers the room is filled with fumes from the stove, but he is incapable of making the effort to arouse himself and to throw open the window. He has lost the will to live. The fortuitous arrival of the sewing woman saves him, and there the novel ends.

We can only speculate that the professor will go on living in isolation amid his family.

IV

What are we to make of this novel—if we can call it a novel? It is a stitching together of two inconclusive fragments about a professor, his family, and his wish for death, and the adventures of a young man alone with the past on a mesa and briefly in touch with the modern urban life of Washington. The two episodes relating to the professor hardly constitute a novel: they convey a picture of his deep depression, which nothing in the book really explains. Why does he wish for death at a time when his life has been crowned with success and when his family flourishes as never before; when indeed there is the promise of a grandchild, for Rosamond expects a baby as the book ends? The Tom Outland story fills in the background of Rosamond's wealth and gives us the strange story of the intense young man who altered the whole course of the professor's life; this does not illuminate, however, the professor's final state of mind. His wish to die is at no point sufficiently motivated by the facts of the small-town life, the general hopelessness of the Philistine surroundings. To believe so intensely in art and the religion of art, and to have created so fully, and yet at the same time to be overpowered by a sense of futility and ineffectuality— these are the contradictions we discern within the professor.

E. K. Brown, in his Alexander Lecture, found an inner unity which he explained in terms of the symbolism of houses within the book. It is a striking passage. There are, he points out, the two houses of the professor, and of these the old house is the significant one. The new house is wrong for him. The Marsellus–Rosamond Norwegian manor house is wrong too. It is a product of pretension and materialism, without regard for the style of the town and the essential dignity of human dwellings. The homes of the Cliff Dwellers—for these are houses also—primitive and wind-swept on their high perch, possessed that dignity. In the third portion of the book the link between these houses is established. Brown continues, speaking of this final part:

> The first and second parts of the book which have seemed so boldly unrelated are brought into a profound unity. It is in this third part of the novel that the large background of emotion, which demands rhythmic expression if we are to respond to it as it deserves, becomes predominant. In the first part it was plain that the professor did not wish to live in his new house, and did not wish to enter into the sere phase of his life correlative with it. At the beginning of the third part it becomes plain that he cannot indefinitely continue to make the old attic study the theatre of his life, that he cannot go on prolonging, or attempting to prolong his prime, the phase of his life correlative with that. The personality of his mature years—the personality that had expressed itself powerfully and in the main happily in his teaching, his scholarship, his love for his wife, his domesticity —is now quickly receding, and nothing new is flowing in. What begins to dominate St. Peter is something akin to the Cliff Dwellers, something primitive which had ruled him long ago when he was a boy on a pioneer farm in the rough Solomon valley in north-

western Kansas. To this primitive being not many things were real; . . . what counted was nature, and nature seen as a web of life, and finally of death.

For the professor remembers an old poem he has read, Longfellow's translation of the Anglo-Saxon *Grave*. He doesn't recall it quite accurately (that is, Miss Cather didn't) but this is what is given in the novel:

> For thee a house was built
> Ere thou wast born;
> For thee a mould was made
> Ere thou of woman camest.

And Brown concludes:

All that had seemed a hanging back from the future—the clinging to the old attic study, the absorption in Tom Outland and the civilization of the Cliff Dwellers, the revival of interest in the occupations of his childhood and its pleasures—was something very unlike what it had seemed. It was profound, unconscious preparation for death, for the last house of the professor.

This seems to me quite admirable literary criticism; the critic has seen the unity of the book created by the central symbol; he has penetrated to the professor's state of mind and grasped that his interest in the occupations of childhood is a stepping backward—or forward—to old age and death. But the story, as told by Miss Cather, in reality leaves the critic helpless in one respect: there is no way to explain why the professor should at this moment of his middle years lose his will to live. We are given no clue. Miss Cather records merely the professor's despair.

V

And now let us apply the tools of psychoanalysis to this material. I want to look at it through the understanding of people and of symbols offered us by Sigmund Freud and, more recently, by Harry Stack Sullivan. The first striking element in the story is the professor's strange attachment to his attic room, high up, old, and cramped, but safely away from the family life in the house below. Now, people do form attachments to rooms and to houses, but the professor's attachment here verges upon the eccentric. He clearly thinks of his attic as a place of—and Miss Cather's words express it—"insulation from the engaging drama of domestic life . . . only a vague sense, generally pleasant, of what went on below came up the narrow stairway." And later he thinks that "on that perilous journey down through the human house, he might lose his mood, his enthusiasm, even his temper."

This is much more than a professor seeking a quiet corner for his working hours. The room is "insulation." The professor withdraws from his family and at the same time makes demands on it, for care, food, attention. There is decidedly something infantile here, the security a baby feels in its possession of the mother and the breast for which it need make no return. In this attic room, tiny and snug as a womb, cradled in a warm and alive household, but safe from any direct contact with the world outside, Professor St. Peter can feel taken care of and as undisturbed as an embryo.

The room, furthermore, is used by one other person —the motherly sewing woman, Augusta. Adjuncts to this mother figure are the two dressmaker's dummies.

Seen as part of the sewing woman, the mother figure, these two dummies express opposite experiences of the mother: one is described as matronly, of a bulk suggesting warm flesh and reassuring physical possession; the other is of sophisticated line suggesting spirit and sexual awareness and interest. So the professor has in his secluded place the beloved mother, who cares for and protects him but is also of some sexual interest to him. He wants his mother to be both a mother and an erotic stimulus and above all he wants to possess her exclusively.

Willa Cather now weaves a second story, but it is in reality a repetition of the same theme. Her hero, again a man, yearns for a high mesa, a sun-beaten plateau, and when he conquers it he finds a cave city. Caves are feminine sexual symbols. These caves are for him inviolate and untouched, like a seemingly virginal mother preserved from others, a mother of long ago, of the infant years, who belonged only to the child greedy at her breast. There is also beautiful pottery. Pottery is again a feminine symbol. The hero cherishes these artifacts and comes to regret that he has a male companion with whom he must share them. The disinclination to share might be seen as sibling jealousy for the mother, or the kind of rivalry a boy, in his Oedipal phase, has for the father who possesses the mother in the sexual way the boy aspires to have her. The hero is disillusioned first when his mother country, symbolized by Washington, is not interested in his discoveries and, in effect, rejects him, and then when his male friend puts the pottery to some practical use: so that we might say the boy is disillusioned when he first learns that in reality his mother is not a virgin and that his father is the cause of her having been thus despoiled. The hero angrily drives the male friend—father or sibling—away and spends a period among the caves—that is with his mother—as blissful as a babe in full possession of the breast. He preserves a record of his narcissistic-infantile paradise, the paradise of life in the womb, of possessing the mother physically, in a notebook which he carefully secretes in the tower. Like the professor's attic room, the tower is still higher and more secluded than the dwellings, where the mother can be preserved, if not in actuality (the pottery), at least in the diary describing his intimate life with her (Outland's detailed account of the caves and their contents as he first found them). Life, its rude events and passage of time, its insistence on moving forward and routing the infant from the womb and the breast, also disrupts the hero's blissful eternity on his hidden mesa, in his caves, with his pottery. He has been disturbed. He seeks stubbornly at least to preserve the memory of days with mother (the mesa, etc.) even as the professor cannot leave his cubbyhole study and would not want the dressmaker's dummies removed.

But life does move on, and in moving on it demands that we follow. The professor seeks a solution to this problem. The family which sustained him in the house below, while he took attic refuge, moves to the new house. If he follows he must accept a new room, a modern room, a room on a lower floor; he must take his place in the family on a different basis; his daughters are now married; they will have children. He must change and grow too, accept his new role as father-in-law and eventually as grandfather. He must, in other words, meet life in an adult way and recognize the demands which are being made on him to take a more active part in the lives of his grown-up children. But the professor clings as long as he can to the old attic room, and with the life gone from the house beneath he is actually threatened with greater isolation than ever before. He has a choice: he can maintain this state of alienation from his family, or he can emerge from his passive dependency and assume the active life expected of him. Appropriately enough, Willa Cather ends her story with the professor nearly suffocating in his room. To remain in the womb beyond one's time is indeed to suffocate. The tenacity of the professor's— and the writer's—determination to maintain this *status quo ante*, if only in fantasy, is illustrated in the ending of the story. It is the sewing woman—who, by the way, was sensibly eager to move to her new, bigger sewing room, to a new life, a new relationship, and cannot understand the professor's infantile attachment to the old room, the old relationship—it is the sewing woman who rescues the professor from suffocation. A mother figure has once more appeared upon the scene for the professor, who thus hangs on to his fixation even though it has brought him an immense threat. The book ends with the professor's problem unresolved, save in the sense that ultimately Mother Earth will enclose him in her womb.

VI

Psychoanalysis, by singling out certain primal elements in the picture, has illuminated our story and offered answers to some of our questions. The professor's death-wish, undefined by the author, would appear to be due to lingering infantile needs, so strong that this successful adult teacher and writer, otherwise a figure of dignity and maturity, adheres to a pattern of behavior which belongs to his childhood. This he masks by rationalization: a love for the past, a dislike of the present. But how are we to handle this material, so heavy with Freud's ideas about infantile sexuality—its insistence upon the attic as a womb symbol, its incestuous fantasies and Oedipal situation—a kind of "psychologizing" which can have meaning only to those who have worked with these concepts on a clinical level? And does this interpretation, fascinating and incredible though some of it is, tell the layman anything about the novel as novel? Or is he being offered a virtually meaningless diagram, highly speculative, of the unconscious fantasies of the professor, derived though it may be from the overt material placed in the book by the author? We all live in some form of house; and doubtless for some of us, on some unconscious level, caves and attics may be wombs and houses mothers, and the smooth curves of pottery may suggest the curves of women. But houses, and the rooms within them, are also universal facts and a universal reality. They testify to man's need for shelter and warmth. It is true that we are thrust out of the womb into the world and must inevitably acquire some shelter, by stages that start with the basket and the cradle and end in adult dwellings. And it is true that there are certain individuals who, instead of welcoming the shelters of this world, long for the unattainable state of the embryo where one was sheltered from everything, that state which James Joyce, mimicking the cradle-tones of our literature, described as "Before born babe bliss had." Wombs are for blissful embryos; houses for growing children and adults. We juggle, so to speak, with the obvious when we invoke such universal symbols.

And what has become of the fine social criticism in

the novel? In tracing such a diagram of the professor's neurosis, it is seen as a mere desire to cling to the past for infantile or infantile-sexual reasons. Yet the social criticism is perhaps the best part of Miss Cather's novels. They record the protest of a gifted woman against the ever increasing conformities and clichés of American life. Her voice is never more resonant than when she shows how the capital of the pioneers was converted into the small change of standardization; and that while the original settlers wrested from the land the glory of America, the sons of the settlers became real-estate agents parcelling this land out and dealing in mortgages, or front-office men—like Louie Marsellus. The anguish of Tom Outland in Washington (whatever neurotic traits he may thereby reveal) is still the genuine anguish of someone who wants government to meet its responsibilities to the past, to history.

And what of criticism of the novel itself? To label the symbols within it in terms of Freud or to describe the "interpersonal" relations between the professor and his family after the manner of Sullivan, gives us no help in assessing the work as work of art. We have merely used psychoanalytic ideas as instruments of quasi-clinical diagnosis. Has Miss Cather successfully carried out her general intention? What is the explanation of the professor's happiness in the past? Why does he experience malaise in the present—a present in which, even without neurotic motivation, the malaise can certainly be held to be genuine?

I have given you the point of view of one critic about this novel, and a psychoanalytical approach to the material. It is my contention that the method used in this approach leads us to a "diagnosis" which can have little meaning unless it is translated into different terms. And I hold that this translation is possible only by calling upon the resources of biography. Let us therefore pursue our inquiry on this third level.

Psychoanalysis is concerned with what goes on in the unconscious and how this is reflected in conscious thoughts and actions. It deals always with a given consciousness. A dream cannot be truly interpreted, as we have seen, unless it is attached to the dreamer, although it may be a pretty story and have distinct meanings for someone to whom it is narrated. These meanings, however, are not necessarily those of the dreamer, who has put into the dream his personal symbols. The personal symbols can be understood only after a close study of their recurrent use in the weaving of that person's dream structures. As with dreams, so with the work of art. Ernest Jones has significantly said:

A work of art is too often regarded as a finished thing-in-itself, something almost independent of the creator's personality, as if little would be learned about the one or the other by connecting the two studies. Informed criticism, however, shows that a correlated study of the two sheds light in both directions, on the inner nature of the composition and on the creative impulse of its author. The two can be separated only at the expense of diminished appreciation, whereas to increase our knowledge of either automatically deepens our understanding of the other.

It is true that sometimes we have no alternative but to cling to our shreds of evidence and to speculate endlessly. But with a writer so recently in our midst as

Willa Cather, we have abundant biographical material relating to her actual experience. We can try to determine—what she at best may have only glimpsed—how this was incorporated into the imagination by which she created.

VII

Our data are derived from E. K. Brown's biography of Willa Cather and from the valuable memoir written by her friend of four decades, Edith Lewis. In these works we discover how intensely Willa Cather suffered as a little girl from an initial displacement from one house to another. She was born in Virginia and lived in a large house. At ten she was torn from the East and taken to the Divide, to a new house. Here she discovered also the sod houses of the early settlers, even as she was later to observe the cave houses of the Cliff Dwellers in the Southwest. We note that the professor in her novel was "dragged" to Kansas from the East when he was eight, that he "nearly died of it."

In Nebraska Willa Cather discovered that nearly all the inhabitants were displaced from somewhere else, and some had been involved in a transatlantic displacement. Her later novels were to depict with deep emotion the meaning of this displacement of the pioneers from Europe and civilization to the rugged prairie. Willa Cather could show empathy with them; their anguish was hers. Then, in Red Cloud, in Nebraska, where the adolescent girl began to discover the life of the frontier, there was a neighboring house in which lived a childless couple. In her own house there was the clash of temperaments and the rivalries of a large family of boys and girls; in their midst was a refined Southern-bred mother, a gentlewoman, somehow strangely aloof and exhausted by repeated pregnancies. And so this other house became a retreat; the cultivated Mrs. Wiener from France served as a kind of second mother to Willa Cather. She provided books and quiet surroundings; the future author could lie for hours on the parlor rug, reading and dreaming. A fairly circumstantial account of the two houses may be found in Miss Cather's late story, "Old Mrs. Harris." From the small town Miss Cather went to Lincoln, Nebraska to attend the university, and here she discovered still another house. It was filled with robust young men, over whom there presided an Old World mother. Miss Cather had again found a home, this time as an escape from the dreariness of a furnished room. The house was that of the Westermann family, and the late William Lynn Westermann of Columbia University, a distinguished Egyptologist, testified to the accuracy of Willa Cather's picture of life in his early home as portrayed in her novel *One of Ours.*

In 1895 Miss Cather went to Pittsburgh and worked on a newspaper. She lived in a series of depressing boarding houses. The way in which she escaped from these into the world of the theater and music is reflected in her ever-popular short story, "Paul's Case." After five years of drab existence she met a young woman who changed the course of her life. This was Isabelle McClung, the daughter of a prominent and wealthy Pittsburgh judge, a strikingly handsome woman interested in the arts. So attached did she become to Willa Cather, the radiance of her personality and the promise of her art, that she invited her to come and live in the McClung family mansion. The gesture might be described as protective and motherly, and

Isabelle became, indeed, during these years, a patron of Miss Cather's art. Her house was many times more elegant and spacious than the Wiener house or the house of the Westermanns. Here Willa Cather put together her first book of verse, began to publish short stories, and finally her first volume of tales. She was given a quiet room to work in at the rear of the McClung mansion. It had been a sewing room. Still standing in it were some dressmaker's dummies.

Willa Cather remained deeply attached to this house. It represented security and peace. From it she was able to face the world and build her career. Even after she had moved to New York and taken up a new abode in Greenwich Village—thus establishing her own home—and was the successful managing editor of *McClure's Magazine,* she would return to Pittsburgh for periodic stays with Isabelle and uninterrupted work in her favorite room.

In the midst of the First World War there came a break. It followed Isabelle McClung's decision to marry a violinist she had known for some years, Jan Hambourg, who with his father and brother had a school of music in Toronto. This happened in 1917 when Miss Cather was in her late forties. Isabelle too was no longer young. Thus a significant change was introduced into the fixed pattern of the years. And it is from this moment that the biographer can date a change in Willa Cather's works. They reflect an increasing tension and deep inner anxiety. Her novel *One of Ours,* written in the early twenties, is an anxious book; on the surface the anxiety is related to the disillusion and malaise that followed the war and to a strong sense of betrayal by the new generation in Nebraska, which was watering down the achievements of the pioneers. For all its defects it won the Pulitzer Prize. The title of the next novel clearly conveys the state of mind of the author: it is the story *A Lost Lady* —and it tells of a woman who clings to a vanished past in a changing world. After this Miss Cather wrote *The Professor's House.*

But just before she set to work on this novel, before she had even had the idea for it, she had gone to France to visit Isabelle and Jan Hambourg. Isabelle, in her French home at Ville-D'Avray, had set aside a study for her friend. The new house would incorporate in it this essential feature of the Pittsburgh mansion. Miss Lewis testifies: "The Hambourgs had hoped that she would make Ville-D'Avray her permanent home. But although the little study was charming, and all the surroundings were attractive, and the Hambourgs themselves devoted and solicitous, she found herself unable to work at Ville-D'Avray. She felt indeed that she would never be able to work there."

Why? Miss Lewis does not tell us. But she does tell us what we already have suspected: that there are some traits of Jan Hambourg in the character of Louie Marsellus. Hambourg was a cultivated musician, deeply read in French literature, and apparently as good a conversationalist as Marsellus. Miss Cather had dedicated *A Lost Lady* to him, thereby welcoming him to the circle of her intimate friends. The strange thing is that she dedicated *The Professor's House* as well: "For Jan, because he likes narrative." As we collate the somewhat pretentious figure of Louie with the figure of the real-life musician, we recover so many similarities, or exaggerations, of certain traits that we are prompted to speculate whether the novelist did not find it necessary to write this flattering dedication—

the second book in succession to bear his name—to miti-
gate the effect of the unflattering portrait she had
painted. A dedication is by its nature so friendly an
act that it is difficult to think of it as masking a
concealed animus. It is clear that Miss Cather was
charmed by one side of Jan Hambourg; but like the
professor, she would have welcomed him as a friend
rather than as the husband of Isabelle-Rosamond.

We can now see what life itself contributed to *The
Professor's House*. Willa Cather's early uprootings have
more meaning in explaining the attachment to a fixed
abode than the universal uprooting from the womb;
her mother's aloofness, and her search for substitute
houses, can also be readily fitted into the novel. The
Pittsburgh house with its sewing room has been transferred into the professor's frame house. Like the professor of her fiction, Miss Cather won a prize during her
middle years; like him, she achieved success. The new
house at Ville-D'Avray has become the new house built
by the professor's family; it too was no substitute for
the old one, since in France Isabelle could no longer
function for Willa Cather as a maternal figure exclusively possessed by her; she now had to share Isabelle
with Jan—as she had had to share her mother with her
brothers; as the professor, though he dislikes it, must
share Rosamond with Louie; and as Outland shares his
caves and pottery with Roddy, only to lose them.

And here we touch the heart of our problem. We
can now see what motivated the depression of Willa
Cather's middle years when she wrote that "the world
broke in two in 1922 or thereabouts," for we know that
to her search for inner security, going back to childhood, was added the deeper sense, irrational from an
adult point of view, that she had been rejected. Of

course this was not so: but our emotions have a way of clinging, in the teeth of adult reality, to patterns fixed at an earlier time. The reality was that Isabelle had moved forward in life, and had married; Willa Cather had not been able to move forward and adapt herself to this situation. In *The Professor's House* Miss Cather had so identified herself with the professor that she could not supply any "rejection motif" for his depression. All she could do was to say that the world was out of joint for him, as it was for herself. This depression of spirit is expressed in her first section, in her account of the professor who cannot keep pace with his family, although his life has been crowned with fame and success.

But such is the nature of our inner fantasies that they persist in seeking expression. In the first part of the novel which emerged from these fantasies, the professor in reality is the one who, by clinging to his attic, has rejected his family. Willa Cather accordingly opens a window into a second theme, after the manner of the Dutch painters, and here she can incorporate her deepest feelings. The Tom Outland story is linked to Isabelle in a curious way. It would seem that in Willa Cather's consciousness the Pittsburgh house, standing on high ground, could be identified with the mesa and the tower. For, some years earlier, when she published *The Song of the Lark*, her first novel to draw upon the Southwest, she dedicated it to Isabelle McClung with the following verses:

> On uplands,
> At morning,
> The world was young, the winds were free;
> A garden fair
> In that blue desert air,
> Its guest invited me to be.

Uplands had become Outland. The world in the "blue desert air" of the mesa is a re-creation of the feeling of freedom Willa Cather had experienced in her life with the maternal Isabelle, patroness of the arts, and in the sewing-room sanctuary of the Pittsburgh mansion. But Tom Outland is rejected twice: the maternal-paternal Government rejects him, and when he returns home he finds that Roddy, his boon companion, has denuded his cliff sanctuary of all that was precious to him. The fantasy of rejection is thus incorporated into the novel.

The Tom Outland story is complete. That of the professor is not. By merging the insights gained from psychology with the biographical data that give us clues to the workings of the author's imagination, we are able to render a critical evaluation: we can see the failure of *The Professor's House* as a work of fiction. The professor lives for us as a man who has given up his good fight and takes the world as preparation for the grave. He has retreated into a vale of misanthropy and despair. He has everything to live for; and for reasons unexplained and unresolved he does not want to live. The materialism of an age, the marrying off of one's children to persons we may like or dislike, the process of growing old—these are not sufficient motives for a depression as deep and as all-consuming as the professor's. The world is never all that we would want it to be, and lives are lived in a constant process of doing, and of ups and downs. The novel is thus incomplete because of Miss Cather's inner problems, which did not permit her to resolve clearly the problems of the character she had projected in her novel. Therefore the professor was not given a clear-cut motivation: his state of mind was described but not explained. The truth was that Willa Cather was incapable of admitting to herself—who can?—that what was troubling her was not the departure of Isabelle but what it symbolized: the reassertion of an old need to have an "other house" and the security of a mother figure all to herself within it. In the guise of Outland, and with a theme further removed from herself, she could project the deeper anxiety resulting from her sense of rejection. The professor was too close to herself. His story could not be told without emotional involvement on the part of the author. Tom Outland was farther away: and his story is told with complete success.

All Willa Cather's later works can be read in the light of this deep feeling of insecurity: her choice of the Rock as the symbol of endurance, her rigidity in the face of her nation's growth and change, her gradual regression in her writings to childhood situations—these spring from the same overpowering isolation, the same death wish yet struggle to live, acted out in the suffocating attic by the professor. I could find other episodes in her life to amplify what I have said. Not least is the one in which she had to uproot herself from her Bank Street apartment in Greenwich Village because a subway was being run through the area. She took refuge for a few days in a lower Fifth Avenue hotel, and remained there for several years. Whatever rationalizations might be offered, it was clearly difficult for her to move and a sheltering hotel, ministering to her needs, seems to have made her reluctant to search out an apartment and re-establish her home. I am told that Miss Cather intensely disliked being in the hotel—all the more reason, we might suppose, for her to have left it sooner than she did. The world did break in two for Miss Cather. One part of it moved on; she remained stranded in the other. And *The Profes-*

sor's House, in its very structure, contained this break. It is an unsymmetrical and unrealized novel because Willa Cather could not bring the two parts of her broken world together again.

To arrive at this view the biographer has had to unite the qualities of critic and psychoanalyst. By penetrating more deeply into the life it has been possible to penetrate more deeply into the work.

By various stages we have now reached the final step which the biographer must take. He has gathered his material and he has interpreted it. Yet a basket of eggs, as Lytton Strachey observed, is not an omelette. The moment has come when the biographer must sit down and write his book. And this by no means simple matter will be the subject of my final discourse.

V Time

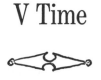

I

In our survey of the biographer's dilemma and the
steps he must take to write a literary life, we now approach the culminating moment. We have watched
him as he chooses his subject; we have tried to accom-
pany him upon his fascinating quest for material; we
have paused to ascertain how he can be a critic alike of
literature and of evidence; and we have sought to determine how he can borrow certain insights from the
sister discipline of psychology, and in particular, from
psychoanalysis. All these necessary steps (and I do not
pretend to have dealt with them exhaustively) are pre-
liminary to the final act. There comes at last a moment
when the biographer must cease the absorbing pursuit
of his helpless subject, when the clutter on his great
worktable which I have repeatedly imaged must take
on some semblance of order, and when, seated behind
it, with blank sheets of paper in front of him, he must
collect his wits and start to write. At this moment the
literary investigator, the critic, the psychologist, become one—the biographer.

It can be an awful moment. Where is the biographer
to begin? How, in that welter of material, amid the

multitudinous months and days of another man's life, is he to find those points of departure which will enable him to proceed on his difficult way? In his mind are a million facts exerting a simultaneous pressure; around him are the notes and files which now must be converted into a readable book; and all this crowded detail must flow from his pen in an orderly fashion and in lucid prose, must be fitted into a narrative, calm and measured and judicial, capable of interesting the reader and conveying to him in some degree the fascination which has kept the biographer for long months at his task.

What kind of biography shall it be? How much of the material shall he use? And in what manner is the story to be told? Biographers do not consciously sit down at the last moment to ask themselves these questions; the questions have been asked before, while they have labored: the answers, however, must be found in the final act of writing. At some point the decision has had to be taken—or will be taken—which will determine the scope of the work and the technique of narration. To some extent the importance of the life that is being written may dictate an answer, and the writing, also, will be profoundly influenced by the quantity and nature of the materials. Thus a commemorative biography or an authorized biography will, by its nature, tend to be envisaged quite differently from a biography written as a result of the biographer's own deep interest in the subject he has selected. Usually, in the latter case, we may expect the biographer to take a more accurate measure of his man, unless he writes with excessive worship or excessive animosity: otherwise he should be able to provide him, so to speak, with a properly fitted suit of clothes.

There are, in biography, as many kinds of garments as there are subjects to wear them, and each garment will have its special cut and its particular frills and decorations. It is not my intention here to imitate Carlyle and to offer you a disquisition upon biographical dress: but you will remember that in the opening pages of *Sartor Resartus* the author observes that "neither in tailoring nor in legislating does man proceed by mere Accident, but the hand is ever guided on by mysterious operations of the mind. In all his Modes, and habilitory endeavours, an Architectural Idea will be found lurking." I think at least three main Architectural Ideas can be found in the structure of biographies. The first and most common is the traditional documentary biography, an integrated work in which the biographer arranges the materials—Boswell did this—so as to allow the voice of the subject to be heard constantly (even when that voice is heard in converse with his own biographer, as in the case of Boswell). The second type of biography is the creation, in words, of something akin to the painter's portrait. Here the picture is somewhat more circumscribed; it is carefully sketched in, and a frame is placed around it. The third type, which has been fashioned increasingly in our time, is one in which the materials are melted down and in which the biographer is present in the work as omniscient narrator. We are given largely, in such a work, the biographer's vision of his subject. The first type of biography might be said to be chronicle; the second pictorial; the third narrative-pictorial or novelistic.

The chronicle life is a large, roomy life in which documents are constantly in the foreground, and the author is never so happy as when he can be quoting liberally from them. Often such works are "official biographies," that is, works designed as standard lives "for the record," and in the circumstance the biographer is inclined, and indeed obliged, to put into his book a great deal more than would be used by other biographers. In a portrait biography, for instance, a principle of high selectivity is inherent in the form; though the portrait-biographer more often than not leans heavily upon official lives, they might be said to represent the entire landscape around a portion of which he will place his frame. For the chronicle life essential background is established; the documents are usually presented in chronological fashion and annotated. Sometimes the background looms very large. Masson's life of Milton is a good example of the "life and times" treatment validly employed in one of the large-dimensioned biographies of our literature, because Milton's life touched its time at so many points. The result is a work of history created around a central figure—and since letters and private papers are given *in extenso,* a heavy autobiographical component is introduced into the biographical creation. Documents, however, are seldom all-revealing and there remains something inevitably arbitrary about the chronicle procedure. It is arbitrary because some letters are preserved through fortuitous circumstances and others disappear. Who is to know whether those preserved are not sometimes the trivial ones and those which have disappeared the important ones? In such a biography no particular attempt is made, usually, to rehearse any portion of the life in dramatic form; if the biographer writing in this fashion has a large sense of life, and is accomplished in the art of expression, he can endow his work with a certain amount of grandeur by the sense of continuity

and completeness, weight and authority it conveys—
for all its inherent incompleteness. The figure is there,
and sometimes it lives because the documents themselves are alive and impart to the orderly text a constant vividness; and sometimes also because the entire
structure breathes the vitality and informing mind of
the biographer as well. The combination of vivid subject and vivid biographer, however, is rare; more often
than not vividness goes a-begging in the hands of
pedestrian but meticulous biographers who, when they
have finished, have merely placed the reader in front
of their well-arranged worktable. Or, to vary the image,
they leave on our hands a frozen statue, cold as marble,
and as sepulchral.

The second biographical type frankly calls itself a
"portrait." When it is actually written as one, not
merely so named, it is something quite different from
the classical chronicle type of biography. It derives in a
sense from those minutes of lives which John Aubrey
recorded in the seventeenth century; it is the biography
of a man in brief; it seeks to catch the essential traits,
all that will characterize and express the personality
and suggest the life *behind* the surface exhibited to the
world; it employs a minimum of background, and, as
in the painting of a portrait, frames the subject in a
given position. The English Men of Letters series, that
splendid though unequal group of literary biographies
first edited by John Morley, contained a number of
well-told lives which, in their concision and adherence
to subject alone, might be considered as "portraits."
And there is that hybrid, also a kind of portrait, which
bears the title *critical biography:* that is, a biography
which seeks to delineate the subject in terms of the
works and by a critical discussion of these is able to

convey some picture of the creating mind or personality. In my opinion, however, such portraits are matters of accident, or approximations of the pictorial life.

The very type and model of the portrait biography in our time, it seems to me, is Geoffrey Scott's *The Portrait of Zélide*, which, after a quarter of a century, bids fair to take its place as a classic example. It is a work compounded of grace and charm; it is written with a rare economy of word and phrase, almost as if each were a brush stroke; the style is inimitable, as good styles are. The portrait is of a vigorous lady of the rational century who scribbled novels at Neuchâtel and whose path was crossed briefly by the peripatetic Boswell and, for a longer period, by a mercurial gentleman who bore the unmercurial name of Constant. If we examine the strokes by which Geoffrey Scott (he was an architect turned man of letters) painted his portrait of Zélide, or, as history better knows her, Madame de Charrière, we see that he had but few documents to draw upon: some bundles of letters, preserved by accident (including a long, fatuous, and extremely droll missive from Boswell); a weighty chronicle life, written by a Neuchâtel professor, essentially archival in character; and the writings of Benjamin Constant and of Madame de Charrière herself. Yet so carefully did Scott read himself into this distant time that Zélide is there before us, all verve and quick intelligence in action or in repose: first as she was in that old house at Zuylen, in Holland, where she was born and "from whose walls innumerable Van Tuylls looked down in stiff disapproval of their too lively descendant," and later in Utrecht or in Paris or in the sleepy manor at Neuchâtel where she, who had scorned the dullness of Holland, finally settled for that long dull married life her mind willed her into, against the better dictates of her heart. "Madame de Charrière," wrote Geoffrey Scott at the beginning of his biographical portrait,

> was not of marble, emphatically, nor even of the hardness of Houdon's clay. But the coldness of Houdon's bust—its touch of aloofness—corresponds to an intellectual ideal, more masculine than feminine, which she set before herself. It embodies a certain harsh clear cult of the reason which at every crisis falsified her life. She was not more reasonable, in the last resort, than the rest of humanity. She paid in full and stoically, the penalty of supposing herself to be so.

The clarity with which Scott sees his characters, placing each in its limited scene, and his capacity—rare among writers and scholars—for reading the emotions in his documents as well as the words, enables him to trace for us with a pen lyrical and psychological the course of two obsessions: Benjamin Constant's and Madame de Charrière's for each other:

> The attraction was between two minds, bewilderingly akin. To each the self-conscious analysis of every pulse and instant of life, of every problem and situation, was as necessary as a vice. Benjamin was a libertine when the mood was on him, just as in other moods he became an ambitious author or a politician; but he was a thinker always; and his intellect never worked with more startling clearness than when his emotions were involved. The thing he shared with Madame de Charrière—this rapid clarity and ceaseless gymnastic of the mind—was not a

mood, but the man himself. Understanding that, holding him by that, she held him as strongly as any woman could.

And Geoffrey Scott is led to the question that all his readers would inevitably ask. Were they then lovers, these two minds? "The subject has its pedantries like any other," Scott writes, "I will not explore them," and he thus forgoes the opportunity for the kind of speculation which certain biographers, M. Maurois for example, would relish. "Psychologically," Geoffrey Scott adds, "the character of their relation is abundantly clear; technically the inquiry would be inconclusive."

Biography is never finer than when it is as candid as this. To the quick sketch for a portrait which Geoffrey Scott draws in the early pages of his work the portrait itself remains loyal, so that we have at the end but the expected culminating point. Belle de Zuylen, Madame de Charrière, awaits death "a frond of flame; a frond of frost." It is tempting to linger with the quiet wit, and the crisp, almost metallic style, as eighteenth-century as its subject, by which Geoffrey Scott brought to life this woman long dead and engaged our interest in her. But we must pass on to further definitions.

I would invoke, however, one more example of a portrait, painted during the recent war years, which, perhaps because of this, has not received the large attention it deserves: Percy Lubbock's *Portrait of Edith Wharton.* It is a portrait drawn with the same concision as that of Zélide, but it is derived from more ample materials; also this time the biographer had known his subject. Lubbock's method, no less urbane and suave than his predecessor's, was to assemble the testimony of Edith Wharton's friends, early and late. We thus see

Mrs. Wharton through a series of "points of view"—a not unexpected device on the part of the author of *The Craft of Fiction*. What these two portraits have in common is their essentially two-dimensional quality, their constant focusing on the central figure. To create a good biographical portrait requires the greatest kind of economy, a constant sensitivity to the materials (or shall we say pigments?), and an eye for all that characterizes and "represents," all that is vivid and human in the subject.

The third type of biography is at once larger than the portrait and yet smaller than the full-length biography. In this kind of biography the documents are seldom quoted at length, but are melted down and refined so that a figure may emerge, a figure in immediate action and against changing backgrounds. Such a work tends to borrow from the methods of the novelist without, however, being fiction. Here the biographer is not concerned with strict chronology; he may shuttle backward and forward in a given life; he may seek to disengage scenes or utilize trivial incidents—which others might discard—to illuminate character; he has so saturated himself with his documents that he may cut himself free from their bondage without cutting himself free from their truth. He achieves this by means wholly selective and psychological.

Lytton Strachey was the father of this kind of biography in our time. He is now under eclipse, and I fear that many of his gifts of style and of insight, as well as his biographical innovations, are overlooked because he allowed his hostility to the Victorians to color much of his work. His animus pervades *Eminent Victorians;* the very title is tinged with irony once we discover what Strachey does to their eminence. And while his biography of Queen Victoria is written with a mellower pen, we are never in doubt that he disapproved of what might be called the Queen's "middle-classness," her rigidities, her sentimentality, her aesthetic blindnesses, those very qualities by which he shows her human and fallible—although a queen. Strachey was a master of biographical irony. Irony, however, can distort as well as it can illuminate, and he became, as a result, the involuntary founder of a whole school of "debunking" biography. His imitators generally ended by writing biographies which criticized the subjects for leading the lives they did; they captured the worst side of Lytton Strachey and overlooked his best: his accurate perception of character and humanity in his personages. Whatever quarrel we may have with his portrait of Victoria and her Consort, we cannot deny the fact that they are living figures—human in the midst of their onerous and often starched responsibilities; they have a vividness which Strachey's imitators seldom achieved. "He maintained," said Edmund Wilson after Strachey's untimely death, "a rare attitude of humility, of astonishment and admiration, before the unpredictable spectacle of life." It is this side of Strachey which is really important now. These are the positive elements in the work of this now underestimated figure, from whom there is still much that we can learn: his genius for squeezing into a single phrase certain aspects of a person; his capacity for combing great masses of documents to find the substance of that phrase; the skill with which he captures incident and detail in order to light up a whole scene or to bring a personality into relief; above all the dazzling qualities in his prose by which he lifted biography from plodding narrative into the realm of literary art. It has been said of him that he was the "supreme and perhaps only example of an artist in fiction who naturally expressed his genius in biography," and Sir Harold Nicolson has testified to the other aspect of him, that side which fervently believed in intellectual honesty, with "an almost revivalist dislike of the second-hand, the complacent, or the conventional; a derisive contempt for emotional opinions . . . a respect, ultimately, for man's unconquerable mind." Sir Harold, I think, does full justice to him; but Strachey's shortcomings have been allowed to tower over his accomplishments, and he has been undone to some extent by his imitators.

And so this third type of biography, striking a middle course between the long, documented life and the portrait, can borrow some of Strachey's theories and methods. In this type the biographer constantly characterizes and comments and analyzes, instead of merely displaying chronologically the contents of a card index or a filing cabinet. "Uninterpreted truth," Strachey said, "is as useless as buried gold; and art is the great interpreter. It alone can unify a vast multitude of facts into a significant whole, clarifying, accentuating, suppressing, and lighting up the dark places of the imagination." Interpretation need not become, however, moral approval or disapproval of the life itself. There enters into the process a quality of sympathy with the subject which is neither forbearance nor adulation; it is quite simply the capacity to be aware at every moment that the subject was human and therefore fallible, and that his having been a writer does not mean that we must demand perfection of him.

II

I now propose to pause, in the midst of these reflections upon the nature of literary biography, to discuss at some length a work of fiction. Novelists have often pretended they were writing biographies or autobiographies. This was the method of Daniel Defoe, that master mingler of truth and fiction; of Dickens in *David Copperfield*, of Sterne in *Tristram Shandy*, the full title of which is *The Life and Opinions of Tristram Shandy, Gentleman*. The particular novel I wish to speak of belongs to this tradition but is markedly different in one respect, for, though it pretends to be a biography, it does not pretend to verisimilitude. The biography which is recounted is that of an individual who lives for more than three centuries. The title is *Orlando: A Biography*. It was written by Virginia Woolf.

One does not have to read far into the work to discover that it is a fantasy in the form of a biography. Orlando's longevity is by no means the only unusual thing about him. He starts out as a youth in the Elizabethan age; he arrives in the Victorian, a young woman. The book begins with a modest and slightly farcical acknowledgment, after the manner of ponderous biographies, in which Mrs. Woolf thanks a great many writers for the help they gave her in composing this work. She lists Defoe, Sir Thomas Browne, Sterne, Scott, Macaulay, Emily Brontë, and others. There are also friendly acknowledgments to two biographers, Lytton Strachey and Harold Nicolson. In keeping with its nature the volume is endowed with an index. The pretense of scholarship and exactitude is maintained to the end. Yet it is a rather mischievous index, for it supplies data not in the text. Thus early in the book Orlando spies, while dashing through the servants' quarters, a rather fat, shabby man, "whose ruff was a thought dirty, and whose clothes were of hodden brown." He has a tankard of ale beside him and paper in front of him and he seems in the act of rolling some thought up and down. "His eyes, globed and clouded like some green stone of curious texture, were fixed." And Orlando, rushing to offer a bowl of rosewater to the great Queen, has only time to wonder whether this man is a poet who could tell him "everything in the whole world." Only in the index do we discover—though we tend to guess it—that the poet was Shakespeare.

Such then are the conventional trappings which dress out this fantasy-biography. Small wonder that Mrs. Woolf was promptly asked by the booksellers whether they were to place the book on the fiction or the biography shelf. Mrs. Woolf had a vision of reduced sales because the book was as ambiguous as the sex of its hero-heroine. She wrote in her diary that it was "a high price to pay for the fun of calling it a biography." She did not have to pay the price. The book sold well on both shelves and it is recognized today as containing some of the novelist's most brilliant writing: there are few pages in modern English literature to equal the prose in which the great frost of the Jacobean age is described, or the coming of the cloud that settles over London and brings with it the nineteenth century.

For criticism, however, there are more pressing questions than the finding of a proper shelf for *Orlando*. What sort of work is it?—a mere literary lark, a

modern allegory, a subtle fable? "The fun of calling it
a biography," Virginia Woolf had written. It was "fun"
then for the writer, and this we can perceive in the gay
and flashing prose and in the way in which the imagination is allowed to romp from the unexpected to the
unexpected. Conventions are mocked, the suffragette
question is treated in a vein of satire, and Mrs. Woolf
tries to remind us throughout the book of the androgy-
nous character of all life. Literary pundits are also
satirized, and so are critics. Biographers are lectured in
long asides on how to write biography; and the book
ranges far and wide in its actual story of Orlando. We
discover him as a youth slashing at the skull of a Moor
in the great house of his ancestors during the reign of
Elizabeth I: he is all fire and poetry and passion. He
falls in love during the reign of James with a Muscovite
princess who is visiting England; at this time the
Thames freezes over and great spectacles and cere-
monies are held on the ice. The princess proves fickle
enough and Orlando tries to mend his broken heart
and find solace in literature. Throughout the book he is
attempting to write a long poem called *The Oak Tree*.
In due course he is named ambassador to Turkey, and
this gives Virginia Woolf an opportunity to mock the
life of high diplomacy. Orlando somewhere along the
way marries a gypsy, Rosina Pepita; and then, after
falling into a trance during a period of riot and massa-
cre, awakens to discover that there has been a great
change. He had gone to sleep an ambassador. He
awakens an ambassadress; but since the embassy is no
more, as a result of the riots, the female Orlando goes
off to live among the gypsies. Homeward bound she
begins to discover how pleasant it is to receive gallant
and even amorous attention from men, and in particu-

lar the ship's captain. When she lands, England has
reached the eighteenth century. There is a great law-
suit to determine her rights to the male Orlando's extensive properties. She pours tea for Addison, for Dr.
Johnson, for Mr. Pope at different times during the
century, but decides they do not really like women.
And so she lives into the century of Victoria, becomes
domestic, falls in love, marries, has a son, and eventually she is riding in trains and driving a car. Having
spanned centuries, Virginia Woolf in the end pinpoints
the moment: it is midnight, 11 October 1928—the
clocks chime the hour and the book ends.

Some critics treated this novel as a sheer extrava-
ganza; others studied it as a serious piece of fiction to
be equated with her other works. Bernard Blackstone,
one of her most sensitive critics, observes that "the
mastery of detail is admirable, and yet we miss the
personal touch, the note of passion and pity which
raised the novels to tragic heights." This judgment
seems to me to mix things up a bit. It ignores, I think,
Virginia Woolf's intention. A close examination of the
book—and indeed the subtitle "A Biography"—suggests
that it was not in reality intended to be a work like
To the Lighthouse or *Mrs. Dalloway* and that it is
wrong to ask of it the passion and pity of the other
books. I discern in this work quite other elements—
qualities satirical and didactic. It seems, in the first
place, to have been intended as a *roman à clé;* the key
is virtually placed by Mrs. Woolf in the reader's hand.
The original edition contained four photographs of Virginia Woolf's intimate friend Vita Sackville-West, and
it was abundantly clear, even from a superficial examination of the work, that in describing the country
house of Orlando with its three hundred and sixty-five

rooms the author had described closely, if in an exaggerated manner, the essential aspects of Knole, the country house of Sir Thomas Sackville and his descendants. The book is in part a pastiche of Sackville family history and a scarcely concealed biographical sketch, genealogy and all, of Vita Sackville-West (to whom it is dedicated). Her grandmother was Pepita, the gypsy, and her grandparents were involved in an elaborate suit over the legitimacy of the children of Lionel Sackville-West and Pepita. Vita Sackville-West is the author of a poem, *The Land,* which is Orlando's poem *The Oak Tree.*

This then is the more overt material in the book. It is equally clear that within it Virginia Woolf was sketching, in a high poetic fashion, the changing temper of English literature and the changing aspects of the English social scene between Elizabethan days and modern times, and the role of the man of letters from the time of Shakespeare to the time of Lytton Strachey. At every turn we discover her nimble imagination pulling together many of the rich threads that have fashioned the contemporary English mind.

If we go outside the book to seek its history, we come upon still more curious matters, a veritable network of biographers. The idea for the work appears to have been given to Virginia Woolf by Lytton Strachey. One day at lunch he told her that he felt she was not yet master of her fictional method—this was apropos of *Mrs. Dalloway.* He suggested (and she put it into her diary): "You should take something wilder and more fantastic, a framework that admits of anything, like *Tristram Shandy.*" This fictional biography thus stems from a pre-eminent figure in modern biography. The acknowledgment, as we have seen, carries not only

Strachey's name, but also that of another biographer, Harold Nicolson, who like Strachey, was one of the band of intellectuals known as the Bloomsbury Group and who was to write a little volume on biography published by Leonard and Virginia Woolf at the Hogarth Press. The plot thickens considerably when we note that Sir Harold Nicolson's wife is none other than Vita Sackville-West. And if we remind ourselves that Virginia Woolf's father, Sir Leslie Stephen, was the editor of the *Dictionary of National Biography,* we have a vision of Orlando in a cradle, grandfathered and uncled by a group of biographers.

Is it any wonder then that imbedded in this would-be biography is a full-fledged theory of biography and that the book seems to be saying a great deal about this art or science or craft—saying it to the shade of Sir Leslie, to Strachey, to Nicolson and using Lady Nicolson's family history as its subject? *Orlando* is in reality neither a literary joke nor entirely a novel: it belongs to another *genre.* It is a fable—a fable for biographers, embodying those views of biography which had often been exchanged among the Bloomsbury Group, but to which are now added a series of commentaries and illustrations by Mrs. Woolf. The work speaks for a looser, freer kind of biography; and it is interesting that in a letter to Lady Nicolson Mrs. Woolf spoke of trying to "revolutionize biography in a night."

Mrs. Woolf hardly started a revolution, but her book has been inviting biographers to read and study it for two decades. *Orlando's* central and gentlest mockery is of time and of history: its insistent theme is that human time does not accord with clock time and that our mechanical way of measuring the hours makes no allowance for the richness of life embodied in a given moment, which can hold within it the experience of decades. Clocks may chime in Edwardian or Georgian England or in the England of Elizabeth II, but they are chiming in an England that was also the England of Elizabeth I. Are there not great houses like Knole still standing with their backward reach to the other time, with rooms in which the present holds the past in a tight embrace? Lady Nicolson's own account of Knole mentions chairs, stools, sofas, love-seats with their original coverings untouched, "but merely softened into greater loveliness by time." She goes on: "They stand beneath the portraits of the men and women who sat in them; the great four-poster beds still stand in the rooms of the men and women who slept in them, drawing the curtains closely round them at night to keep out the cold. The very hairbrushes are still on the dressing tables"; and the very people of today, like Vita Sackville-West, is not their backward reach to the ancestry that lived in such a house as close and as real? And does not this mean that the biography of any individual must be re-created out of a total past and not merely out of the mechanical calendar present of their lives? It is by this route that we come to an even deeper level in *Orlando:* for while Virginia Woolf attached her story to fragments from the life of her friend Lady Nicolson, what she is telling us also in this book is the story of her own life. She appears to be saying that when she was young and at liberty in Sir Leslie Stephen's great library her imaginative life was identified with the Elizabethans; she too could experience the vigorous sensual life of the age, glimpsing the great figures and winning favor at the court of Elizabeth; all her readings of the old writers had so much reality for her that they came to be a part of her own life. Perhaps *she* had slashed at the head of a Moor and had adventures on the frozen Thames and loved a beautiful princess from Muscovy. Then, growing older, she was disturbed as a young woman by the tyranny of sex when she found herself at large in a man's world. At the same time she was an individual who had absorbed her nation's literature and traditions and this made her one with her land. She was England and all that it had been. In this sense may not an artist transcend his sex when he embodies within him, and speaks for, his nation's cultural and historical heritage? May not the artist possess instead of mere femininity or masculinity the very stuff and fiber of a people, indeed both the masculine and the feminine qualities of England's greatness? A biographer attempting to deal strictly with the facts of Virginia Woolf's life would miss this rich fabric woven into the deepest parts of her consciousness, past and present, and would reduce her to a line drawing or a caricature rather than capture the many selves of which she was the composite.

What are some of the asides in *Orlando* on the subject of biography? I have already quoted a few: "that riot and confusion of the passions and emotions which every good biographer detests"—this is but one of Mrs. Woolf's many jibes at conventional biographers. At another moment she suggests that a biographer must keep pace with the development of the personality he is re-creating; she wonders also whether this can really be accomplished; it involves keeping pace not only with an individual but with those many selves which we are within our constituted self. She speaks of the "first duty of a biographer" and mockingly describes it as "to plod without looking to right or left, in the indelible footprints of truth; unenticed by flowers; regardless of shade, on and on methodically"—and here she echoes Strachey—"till we fall plump into the grave and write finis on the tombstone above our heads." (Strachey's passage, in the preface to *Eminent Victorians,* has been quoted many times and yet I cannot resist repeating it at this point: "With us," wrote Strachey of Victorian biography, "the most delicate and humane of all the branches of the art of writing has been relegated to the journeymen of letters; we do not reflect that it is perhaps as difficult to write a good life as to live one." And he continued: "Those two fat volumes, with which it is our custom to commemorate the dead—who does not know them, with their ill-digested masses of material, their slipshod style, their tone of tedious panegyric, their lamentable lack of selection, of detachment, of design. They are as familiar as the cortege of the undertaker, and wear the same air of slow, funereal barbarism.")

Virginia Woolf in *Orlando* seems to have Strachey constantly in mind. The biographer, she says, is a votary of Truth, Candor and Honesty, "the austere Gods who keep watch and ward by the inkpot of biography," and at the moment of Orlando's change of sex these three engage in a duel with Purity, Modesty and Chastity. Their insistent trumpetings that the truth be told finally prevail. Later we discover that biographers and historians in Mrs. Woolf's view are not capable of writing truthful accounts of London society, "for only those who have little need of the truth and no respect for it—the poets and the novelists—can be trusted to do it, for this is one of the cases where the truth does not exist." The undercurrent of Mrs. Woolf's argument is that we live in a solipsistic universe and that the only truth we know is that which lies within the envelope of personal consciousness. To the attempt to describe this evanescent universe she is wholly dedicated. There are passages in *Orlando* on the sexlessness of biographers and historians, on the helplessness of the biographer before thought and emotion in his subject, on the biographical reliance on the words "perhaps" and "it appears"—and when we have made our way through the book and added up these numerous asides we must recognize that at the heart of Virginia Woolf's argument is the question of time. Here she is at one with all her contemporaries—those who have written novels since Bergson—Proust and Joyce, Dorothy Richardson and William Faulkner. What they have tried to do in fiction, that is, record man's sense of time, psychological and human, as distinct from clock time, she feels to be an attempt that belongs also to the field of biography. She writes in *Orlando:*

An hour, once it lodges in the queer element of the human spirit, may be stretched to fifty or a hundred times its clock length; on the other hand, an hour may be accurately represented on the timepiece of the mind by one second. This extraordinary discrepancy between time on the clock and time in the mind is less known than it should be and deserves fuller investigation. But the biographer, whose interests are, as we have said, highly restricted, must confine himself to one simple statement: when a man has reached the age of thirty, as Orlando now had, time when he is thinking becomes inordinately long; time when he is doing becomes inordinately short. Thus Orlando gave his orders and did the business of his vast estates in a flash; but directly he was alone on the mound under the oak tree, the seconds began to round and fill until it seemed as if they would never fall.

So far as I am aware, no biographers have listened to the fable Virginia Woolf created for them—a work whimsical, and mocking, and idiosyncratic, and yet filled with many wonderful flashes of truth—because *Orlando* belongs to the shelf of fiction! It is clear that the biographer cannot do all that Mrs. Woolf wants him to do—he can never penetrate to the consciousness of his subject, he can only guess at his thoughts and only suggest the successive days of his life. But he can do much more than he has been doing. It is an ironic footnote to *Orlando* that when Virginia Woolf did write a genuine biography, a life of Roger Fry, the art critic, she did not succeed in being half as evocative or as lively as in her fictitious biography of Orlando. The Fry biography has certain very fine passages in which Mrs. Woolf writes out of her own Bloomsbury Group memories; but the total effect of the book is rather wooden, perhaps because it is difficult to write the life of a critic without getting involved in many critical ideas; and these ideas can impart to such a life an intellectual rather than emotional effect and even a certain aridity. At the same time we must recognize that the book was a commemorative biography, suffering from connections and emotions that touched Mrs. Woolf's own life closely. Above all we must recognize that there is no discipline less congenial to a novelist than that of having to write imaginatively about facts instead of imagining the facts themselves. I suspect that a student of biography, seeking to understand something about that art, would do well to read not the life of Roger Fry, sound, careful, honest, sensitive though it is, but the soaring and playful, yet highly serious and didactic—if fictitious—*Orlando*.

III

I have no argument with Virginia Woolf on the question of time: attach a biography to mechanical time and you run the risk of having a mechanical biography. Yet many of our biographies suffer from this defect: written chronologically, they do not suggest the human element of time in a life, the fact that on a given day we relive whole parts of our past, and that there is always an interplay between past and present. A chronological biography runs the risk of flattening out a life and giving it the effect of a calendar or a date book. Sometimes, however, this method is called for by the material. Rupert Hart-Davis, in his admirable study of Hugh Walpole, by giving us the recurrent pattern, year by year, of Walpole's life, has made vivid for us how that skillful storyteller lived out a success story—as if life were an engagement book. On the other hand, I have read several biographies recently in which the year-in-year-out formula isolates episodes and ideas, scatters them through the years, when they should have been brought together. I think, however, that it is best here not to discuss theory but to find illustration, and I shall describe how I plan to write a certain chapter in the second volume of the life of Henry James, upon which I am now engaged. The point of my example is that biography can violate chronology without doing violence to truth.

In scanning Henry James's life during the years that

followed his first adult journey to Europe, I came upon the following sentence in an unpublished letter to Grace Norton, his Cambridge friend. "I spent lately," wrote the future novelist, "a couple of days with Mr. Emerson at Concord—pleasantly but with slender profit." That is all. Were I writing the chronicle type of biography I would quote this at the proper calendar date, September 1870. This would convey to the reader the simple historical fact: the future novelist spent a couple of days—slenderly profitable—with the great Ralph Waldo Emerson in his Concordian setting. Two years later in my chronicle I would mention that Henry James met Mr. Emerson in Paris. They visited the Louvre together. A few months later I would report that they met in Rome. They spent a morning together looking at the sculptures in the Vatican. When I reach the year 1883, when Henry James has become famous, I would chronicle the fact that he journeys once again to Concord, this time to attend Mr. Emerson's funeral. And in my chronicle I would in due course mention James's reviews of the Carlyle-Emerson correspondence in 1883 and describe an article on Emerson which James published in December of 1887.

Why did James write this article in the year 1887? It was not because at this moment he felt prompted to recapture the image of his departed friend. There was a fortuitous circumstance. The essay was occasioned by the publication of the Cabot life of Emerson. Although James was writing it in 1887, his actual relationship with his subject belongs, as we have seen, to an earlier period. Yet the chronicle biography would deal with the essay under 1887, validly enough, although the date is an accidental one. On the other hand, when James visited Emerson in Concord seventeen years before, he was in relation with a man he had known from his early childhood, whose work he had read and admired. He had heard him lecture; he was familiar with his life at Concord; he had met or known through Henry James Senior some of the men and women who surrounded Emerson. Emerson thus was not merely an august figure in the life of Henry James, an elder man of letters. He was woven into the fabric of James's consciousness and into James's life, not at the precise chronological moments that I happen to know about because certain records have been preserved; there were many other moments, moments perhaps of greater importance, for which we do not have the record. He is represented in James's life not only as a figure encountered now and again during four decades but as a veritable symbol, a revered and noble presence, a voice rich with the many tones of New England. When they went to look at the pictures in the Louvre, there was, in the consciousness of James an increasingly composite figure, which was the Emerson of all the years he had known him—the Emerson in his prime, the Emerson in his old age. And when the final respects were paid to him at the grave, a summarized Emerson existed in his mind whom he could evoke, piecing together the Emerson of his memories: the benevolent, sparse figure of the 14th Street hearthside, the man who read his Boston Hymn at the moment of the emancipation of the slaves, the rural figure in his homely setting—indeed the man in all the decades as Henry James had known him. Now, what was important for James: these pleasant encounters, of which there may have been many more than we know, or the man and what he stood for, and his work, to which James returned at various times with unmistakable pleasure, and the qualities, as well as the defects, he discerned in the eminent personality?

The essay of 1887 gives us the picture. I shall string together a few random sentences. "Emerson's personal history is condensed into a single word Concord, and all the condensation in the world will not make it look rich. . . . Passions, alternations, affairs, adventures had absolutely no part in it. It stretched itself out in enviable quiet—a quiet in which we hear the jotting of the pencil in the notebook. . . . The plain, God-fearing, practical society which surrounded him was not fertile in variations. On three occasions later—three journeys to Europe—he was introduced to a more complicated world; but his spirit, his moral taste, as it were, abode always within the undecorated walls of his youth. There he could dwell with that ripe unconsciousness of evil which is one of the most beautiful signs by which we know him."

There are many more such sentences in the essay, and if we read them, and read between the lines, they tell us much of Henry James's observation of Emerson and his feelings for him and his surroundings. And they tell us much about Henry James, for we see the values and the judgments James invoked in assessing Emerson's role in American life and letters. How much of James's own awareness is implied in that phrase about Emerson's "ripe unconsciousness of evil" for instance! We are provided with ample material to enable us to evaluate the friendship, to form a picture in our mind, and even to create a biographical scene. In my mind all this material melts together into a portrait of the two, the young man and the old, the one at the beginning of his career, the other near the end, in Concord, at the Louvre, at the Vatican. I can place my scene in

Concord in 1870—for this is where Emerson belonged and where both can best be placed in their American setting. In that scene is James, young, earnest, brimming over with his recent European journey; Emerson, old, but not yet suffering from the amnesia of his later years, moving in his contrasted world, the fields and orchards of Concord. In creating this scene I violate no fact. I put no thoughts into James's head or into Emerson's. I adhere to the one point of view in my possession, James's, and try to set down his vision and perception—which he recorded—of the man of Concord. But from Concord I leap into the future, to Europe and back again, and to the past, and back again, and to the funeral, and to Concord again as Henry James viewed it when he himself was old, thirty-five years later, and long after it had taken its cherished place in American literary history. Henry James wrote in 1907 that "not a russet leaf fell for me, while I was there, but fell with an Emersonian drop."

I do this in violation of all chronology, dealing with my subject's relation to Emerson at the most meaningful moment that I can find—the moment when Henry James is taking the measure of America and deciding whether he will remain in that country or yield to his cosmopolitanism. Instead of chronicling little episodes and encounters piecemeal, as mere anecdotes, I recreate two personalities in their relationship to one another and in particular the significance of the older man for the younger. By weaving backward and forward in time and even dipping into the future, which to us, as readers, is after all entirely of the past, I reckon with time, as it really exists, as something fluid and irregular and with memory as something alive and flickering and evanescent. I refuse to be fettered by the clock and the calendar. I neither depart from my documents nor do I disparage them. Ultimately I, as the biographer, must paint the portrait and I can paint it only from the angle of vision I have, and from my time and its relation to the time that I seek to recover. If I paint carefully, and do my utmost not to falsify the colors, there is no reason why I should not in the end be able to hang before my reader a reasonable likeness, which is all that a biographer can hope to achieve—instead of offering him a card index, a cluttered worktable, or a figure of papier-mâché.

I V

The scenic method in literary biography recommends itself to us for a number of reasons and largely because, in addition to being a dramatic method, it enables us to convey more easily the passage of time. As we construct scene after scene, each composed of those moments which we can document, we gain the sense of being in a continuum instead of in separated moments. It is a little like the sense a person may have if he is accustomed to going to the same place every summer, of having been in that place continuously for a long time. What happens is that the intervening winter months fade away and the successive summers become hooked together, melting into one another. The biographical edifice stands much more firmly when it is built in this fashion; the biographer does not indulge in the false pretense of reconstructing every minute, but instead creates a time-atmosphere akin to that created by the novelist. The more loosely written work offers bits and scraps of fact and quotations from documents without any genuine integration of them. The biographer happens to know that a poet saw his mistress on one day, went hunting on the next, mourned at the burial of his favorite hound, and then wrote a letter sympathizing with a friend who had a death in his family. A chronological recital of these facts reads like a newspaper; we jump from one item to another, and the items seem unrelated. But if the story about the mistress is assembled in one place; if at the right moment we glimpse the poet as huntsman or as animal lover, and if we see him in his relationships with his friends, we give to his life a dramatic quality rather than offering a recital of little disconnected facts.

In a sense what I am proposing is that the biographer borrow some of the techniques of fiction without lapsing into fictional biography. A tedious recital of biographical data may still have much life in it when the subject offers a rich mind and an abundance of rich quotation; but it also makes us all the more aware of how much vividness can be lost in the process. What happens often is that the scholar who has carried out the research is not necessarily a writer and lacks the style and the touch that can do justice to his subject. Devotion to the art of expression is needed, and it quite often does not match the devotion to the search for biographical truth. The best one can hope for in such cases is a sober massing of the data, and at least a genuine organization of it. The book then becomes a source book for another and more expert writer who will ultimately be master of this material rather than mastered by it.

On the subject of biography and the novel André Maurois had many interesting things to say in his Clark Lectures. Having written fiction and fictionalized biography before he became a serious biographer, he appreciated the need for striking a balance between the novelist's imaginative freedom and the biographer's factual boundaries. But he saw also what few biographers see, that there is such a thing as finding the ideal form for this factual material. Maurois observes that in *War and Peace*, Tolstoy is able to give Napoleon a vividness he cannot have in the pages of history. Writing as a novelist, not as an historian, Tolstoy can describe Napoleon stretching out his small, chubby hand or casting a glance at the Tsar, impart to him moments of emotion and relationships with various personages utterly impossible to the historian. Particular vividness is obtained, however, because at certain moments we see Napoleon, in this novel, through the eyes of characters such as Prince Andrey; and if we have achieved empathy with the Prince, it is almost as if *we* were looking at Napoleon.

This is a highly suggestive thought. Why should not biographers weigh with great care experiments in "point of view"? Why should they not find, if possible, various angles of vision, so that their subject, instead of being flattened out, attains a three-dimensional quality? I have already mentioned that Percy Lubbock achieved this by showing us Edith Wharton through the eyes of her friends; but such imaginative examples in biographical portraiture are rare. Nevertheless they are more possible to us today because we have much more material from which to fashion them. Biography, in its fear of fiction, has not studied sufficiently, it seems to me, the possible technical borrowings it can make from that characteristic literary form. There remains much room for trial and experiment.

V

And now let us look over the road we have traveled. We have seen that modern literary biography is a delicate and humane process of great complexity, as complex as life itself, involving wide-ranging curiosity and search, critical analysis, psychological insight and a quality of sympathy between biographer and subject— between the hunter and the hunted—all in the interest of truth, truth of life and of experience. I hope that this does not magnify the biographer into something superhuman: to accomplish his task he needs above all to be a serious and painstaking questioner—in a word, an honest scholar; and it is fortunate if he can be an imaginative one as well. In a century such as ours, filled with chaos and violence, he must cling to the high values of civilization and the highest value conceived by the democratic ideal—the sense of the worth and importance of the individual in a world that for all its egalitarian principles still tends to hold life cheap, as witness our chronic wars and the desperate gambles of modern statesmanship. It has been said that what distinguishes man from beast above all is his historic sense, his capacity for remembering rather than living wholly in the present, in other words, his deep sense of life as a continuum, no matter at what moment he happens to have arrived on this earth. Writers have this sense in the greatest degree: and when we write their lives we write also the history of our culture and of our civilization. James Joyce has shown us how the whole history of man is crammed into a single day. When we write the history of *a* man we seek to arrive at some deeper understanding of this process; and when we identify ourselves with such an individual we are learning, in our time, to understand ourselves. Know thyself, the philosopher said; and the biographer seems to say also, "Understand thy neighbor and thou wilt know thyself."

"By telling us the true facts," said Virginia Woolf, "by sifting the little from the big, and shaping the whole so that we perceive the outline, the biographer does more to stimulate the imagination than any poet or novelist save the very greatest. For few poets and novelists are capable of that high degree of tension which gives us reality. But almost any biographer, if he respects facts, can give us much more than another fact to add to our collection. He can give us the creative fact; the fertile fact; the fact that suggests and engenders. Of this, too, there is certain proof. For how often, when a biography is read and tossed aside, some scene remains bright, some figure lives on in the depths of the mind, and causes us, when we read a poem or a novel, to feel a start of recognition, as if we remembered something that we had known before."

A biographer cannot but be grateful when he hears a novelist say this. It reinforces his own feeling that when he has penetrated to the heart of his materials, he throws open a window upon *a* life and thereby opens it upon life itself. Endless are the views and vistas. And I would say that we can sum up the process of gaining such a view in three simple words: understanding, sympathy, illumination.

Notes

I SUBJECT

p. 1. Lytton Strachey's preface to *Eminent Victorians* (London, 1918) contains an admirable, and much-quoted statement on biography. One might consider it, almost, a manifesto for modern biography. His miscellaneous essays and book reviews also contain many suggestive ideas on the biographical art.

p. 5. Two valuable books on early English biography exist, both by the late Donald O. Stauffer: *English Biography before 1700* (Cambridge, Mass., 1930) and *The Art of Biography in 18th Century England* (Princeton, N.J., 1941; two vols.). Edgar Johnson's survey, *One Mighty Torrent,* originally published in New York in 1937 and republished in 1955, includes autobiography, memoirs, diaries, and letters. A valuable study by Wayne Shumaker is *English Autobiography: Its Emergence, Materials and Form* (Berkeley, Calif., 1954).

p. 6. Harold Nicolson, *The Development of English Biography,* Hogarth Lectures, No. 4 (London, 1927). André Maurois's *Aspects de la biographie* (Paris, 1928) contains the six Clark Lectures he delivered at Cambridge University during May 1928. A later statement of M. Maurois's views appeared in the *New York Times Book Review* titled "To Make a Man Come Alive Again" (27 December 1953).

pp. 6–7. Nicolson, *English Biography,* pp. 154–57 discusses the future of biography.

p. 8. Maurois, *Aspects de la biographie,* pp. 107–8.

157

NOTES

pp. 10–11. Sigmund Freud, *Leonardo da Vinci,* tr. by A. A. Brill (New York, 1947), pp. 111–12.

p. 11. Strachey, preface to *Eminent Victorians.*

pp. 13–15. Henry James's *Essays in London* (London and New York, 1893) contains the essay on James Russell Lowell. It is reprinted in *The American Essays of Henry James* (New York, 1956).

p. 16. James Boswell, *The Life of Samuel Johnson L.L.D.* My quotations are from the Oxford edition (London, 1904).

pp. 17–18. For the Young episode see Boswell II, pp. 420–22.

p. 19. Boswell II, pp. 118–19.

pp. 20–21. For the discussion of literary lives see Boswell II, p. 405.

pp. 21–22. For the 1776 journey see Boswell II, pp. 3–4.

p. 24. Beerbohm, Max, "Lytton Strachey," The Rede Lecture, (Cambridge, 1943), pp. 12–13.

II QUEST

pp. 27–29. A. J. A. Symons, *The Quest for Corvo* (1934).

p. 29. T. S. Eliot, *The Three Voices of Poetry* (London, 1954).

p. 30. I am indebted to Prof. William A. Jackson, the librarian of the Houghton Library at Harvard, for the facts about the Wolfe papers.

p. 31. Norman Holmes Pearson, "Problems of Literary Executorship," in *Studies in Bibliography,* Papers of the Bibliographical Society, University of Virginia, V (1952–53). Hervey Allen's letter is on p. 10.

pp. 33–35. Henry James's letters: for a full discussion of James's epistolary habits see *The Selected Letters of Henry James,* ed. L. Edel (New York, 1955; London, 1956).

p. 37. "Approaches to their privacy." In Henry James's review of Hawthorne's French and Italian Journals, the *Na-*

tion (14 March 1872), reprinted in *The American Essays of Henry James.* Also the "Ellery Channing and Lucy Aitken Correspondence" in the *Atlantic Monthly* (March 1875).

p. 37. I am indebted to Mr. Dan H. Laurence for details of the secret drawer in James's desk.

p. 38. The quotations are from various unpublished letters of Henry James. The account of the burning of his papers is from an unpublished letter to Mrs. J. T. Fields, 2 January 1910.

pp. 39–40. Henry James's essay on George Sand, the first of three on the French novelist, appears in *Notes on Novelists* (1914), pp. 168–69 in the American edition and 133–34 in the London edition.

pp. 41–42. Sir James Mackenzie, *Angina Pectoris* (Oxford, 1923), pp. 209–10: "Case 97. Male. Aged 66. Examined 25 Feb. 1909." The unpublished letter from Sir James to Dr. Harold Rypins is dated 12 January 1925, one week before the physician's death. See also R. MacNair Wilson, *The Beloved Physician: Sir James Mackenzie* (London, 1926), p. 49. A posthumous paper on Mackenzie and James by Dr. Rypins was edited by me and appeared in *American Literature,* entitled "Henry James in Harley Street," XXIV, no. 4 (Jan. 1953), pp. 481–92.

p. 43. "Nothing would induce me." Henry James, *Notes of a Son and Brother* (New York and London, 1914), chap. X.

p. 44. "Blood and thunder tale." G. W. James to his parents. See *Alice James: Her Brothers, Her Journal* (New York, 1934), p. 36.

p. 44. T. S. Perry on the young Henry James. See *The Letters of Henry James* (New York and London, 1920), ed. P. Lubbock. In his introduction Mr. Lubbock quotes a memorandum from Perry: "He was continually writing stories, mainly of a romantic kind. The heroes were for the most part villains, but they were white lambs by the side of the sophisticated heroines, who seemed to have read all Balzac in the cradle and to be positively dripping with lurid crimes."

p. 45. "Avowed authorship." Virginia Harlow, *Thomas Sergeant Perry* (Durham, N.C., 1950), pp. 272–73.

p. 46. Mrs. John Hall Wheelock of New York generously read through her grandmother's letters to her father, the writer and critic, Charles De Kay. The passage in the letter of 29 February 1864 reads: "Miss Elly Temple has just come in looking very fresh and pretty—Henry James has published a story in the February Continental, called a Tragedy of Errors. read it. Smith v[an] Buren forbade Ellie to read it! which brought a smile of quiet contempt to Harry's lips but anger and indignation to those of Miss Minnie Temple." Elly and Minnie Temple were Henry James's cousins. Smith Van Buren, a son of U.S. President Martin Van Buren, had married into the James family and was therefore an uncle of the Temple girls and of Henry James.

pp. 46–49. "A Tragedy of Error" appears unsigned in the *Continental Monthly,* a journal "devoted to literature and national policy," V (Feb. 1864), no. 2, pp. 204–16. The editor of the journal at the time the story appeared was Mrs. Martha Elizabeth Duncan Walker Cook. One of the main purposes of the magazine was "to advocate emancipation as a political necessity." For my discussion of the story see *Henry James: The Untried Years* (New York and London, 1953), the chapter titled "Ashburton Place." The story was reprinted in the *New England Quarterly,* XXIX, no. 3 (Sept. 1956) with a prefatory note by me.

III CRITICISM

p. 54. Virginia Woolf, *Orlando* (London and New York, 1928), pp. 189–90.

p. 55. Henry James, in his review of Ernest Daudet's

Mon Frère et moi, Atlantic Monthly, XLIX (June 1882), pp. 846–51.

p. 57. W. B. Yeats, *Autobiographies* (London and New York, 1955), p. 505. See also "William Butler Yeats" by Marion Witt in *English Institute Essays 1946* (New York, 1947), pp. 74–101.

p. 58. *Orlando*, pp. 17–18.

pp. 59–62. F. C. Green, *Jean Jacques Rousseau* (Cambridge, England, 1955). The Vincennes episode is dealt with on pp. 98 *et seq.*

p. 62. Douglas Bush, "John Milton," *English Institute Essays 1946*, pp. 5–19.

pp. 62–63. Cleanth Brooks, foreword to *Critiques and Essays in Criticism* (New York, 1949), p. xix. See also "The Historical Criticism of Milton," by A. S. P. Woodhouse, and "Milton and Critical Re-estimates," by Cleanth Brooks, *PMLA*, LXVI, no. 6 (Dec. 1951), pp. 1033–54.

p. 63. T. S. Eliot, "The Function of Criticism" (1923), in *Selected Essays* (New York, 1932).

pp. 63–64. Frank H. Ellis, "Gray's Elegy: The Biographical Problem in Literary Criticism," *PMLA*, LXVI, no. 6 (Dec. 1951), pp. 971–1008.

p. 65. Mr. Ellis, in criticizing David Cecil's *Two Quiet Lives* (London, 1948), quotes Cecil's passage (p. 136) on Gray's wandering one evening into the churchyard at Stoke Poges and pondering his poem, but omits this significant sentence: "Thus, in sculptured phrase, and grave tolling music, spoke themselves forth *the deepest conclusions borne in on Gray from twenty-six years of troubled life.*" (My italics.)

p. 67. Joseph Wood Krutch, introduction to *The Selected Letters of Thomas Gray* (New York, 1952).

p. 69. C. A. Sainte-Beuve, *Nouveaux Lundis*, III (Paris, 1865): "La littérature, la production littéraire, n'est point pour moi distincte ou du moins séparable du reste de l'homme et de l'organisation; je puis goûter une œuvre, mais il m'est difficile de la juger indépendamment de la connaissance de l'homme même; et je dirais volontiers: *tel arbre, tel fruit.* L'étude littéraire me mène ainsi tout naturellement à l'étude morale."

pp. 72–89. I am much indebted for my discussion of T. S. Eliot's work to Helen Gardner's admirable critical study, *The Art of T. S. Eliot,* 1950.

IV PSYCHOANALYSIS

p. 94. Lionel Trilling, "Art and Neurosis," in *The Liberal Imagination* (New York, 1950).

p. 95. "Triumphs of art over neurosis." Leon Edel, *The Psychological Novel 1900–1950* (London and New York, 1955); *The Letters of Henry James,* ed. P. Lubbock, II, James to Wells, 10 July 1915.

p. 99. E. K. Brown, *Rhythm in the Novel* (Toronto, 1950), pp. 71–78.

p. 100. E. K. Brown, *Willa Cather: A Critical Biography,* completed by Leon Edel (New York, 1953), pp. 238–47.

p. 107. Harry Stack Sullivan (1892–1949), one of the most original psychoanalysts of the American school, who developed the theory of "inter-personal relations" and founded the William Alanson White Psychological Foundation. His theories are recorded in certain of his lectures published posthumously, notably in *The Inter-personal Theory of Psychiatry* (New York, 1953).

p. 114. Edith Lewis, *Willa Cather Living* (New York, 1953), p. 131.

V TIME

pp. 128–30. Geoffrey Scott, *The Portrait of Zélide* (London, 1925).

pp. 130–31. Percy Lubbock, *Portrait of Edith Wharton* (New York, 1947).

pp. 134–45. *Orlando* (London and New York, 1928), pp. 62, 91–93, 123, 174–75, 189–90, 277.

p. 138. Virginia Woolf, *A Writer's Diary* (London and New York, 1953), pp. 79, 113–14, 116–17.

p. 140. Knole and Vita Sackville-West. Aileen Pippett, *The Moth and the Star: A Biography of Virginia Woolf* (Boston, 1955), chap. xiv. See also Frank Baldanza, "Orlando and the Sackvilles," *PMLA*, LXX, no. 1 (March 1955), pp. 274–79.

p. 145. Virginia Woolf, *Roger Fry: A Biography* (London and New York, 1940); Rupert Hart-Davis, *Hugh Walpole: A Biography* (London and New York, 1952).

p. 146. Henry James to Grace Norton, 26 September 1870, unpublished letter in the Houghton Library, Harvard University.

p. 146. Ralph L. Rusk, *The Life of Ralph Waldo Emerson* (New York, 1949). See also Henry James, *Italian Hours* (Boston, 1909), p. 293.

pp. 147–48. Henry James, "The Correspondence of Carlyle and Emerson," *Century Magazine*, XXVI (July), pp. 384–95. "The Life of Emerson" (review of James Elliot Cabot's *A Memoir of Ralph Waldo Emerson*), *Macmillan's Magazine*, LVII (Dec. 1887), pp. 86–98, reprinted under the title "Emerson" in *Partial Portraits* (1888).

p. 154. Virginia Woolf, "The Art of Biography," in *Atlantic Monthly*, CLXIII (April 1939), pp. 506–10. Reprinted in *The Death of the Moth* (1942).

Index

167